A DRUNKS TALE

FROM A LIVING HELL TO FREEDOM

A Message of Hope for Alcoholics and Their Families

FRANK K

authorHOUSE®

AuthorHouse™
1663 Liberty Drive
Bloomington, IN 47403
www.authorhouse.com
Phone: 1 (800) 839-8640

Published by AuthorHouse 05/13/2015

ISBN: 978-1-5049-1063-7 (sc)
ISBN: 978-1-5049-1064-4 (hc)
ISBN: 978-1-5049-1062-0 (e)

Library of Congress Control Number: 2015907268

Print information available on the last page.

Any people depicted in stock imagery provided by Thinkstock are models,
and such images are being used for illustrative purposes only.
Certain stock imagery © Thinkstock.

This book is printed on acid-free paper.

Because of the dynamic nature of the Internet, any web addresses or
links contained in this book may have changed since publication and may
no longer be valid. The views expressed in this work are solely those
of the author and do not necessarily reflect the views of the publisher,
and the publisher hereby disclaims any responsibility for them.

Reprinted from Alcoholics Anonymous,
59-60 with permission from A.A. World Services Inc.

This book is dedicated to all who suffer from the disease of alcoholism and all the families that have been equally hurt by this insidious disease.

The Abyss

I have stood at the gates of a personal hell, lost in a downward spiral. I looked up from the abyss at what was seemingly an insurmountable climb to a place that I wasn't sure existed. I was gazing at a strange world with normal, happy, well-adjusted people, a foreign world in which I didn't fit. I was a drunk, an alcoholic who drank to live and lived to drink. Drinking was my only means to function, and drinking was the only way not to get sick. Drinking was killing me, and yet every ounce of my being told me I had to drink. I was alone in my disease and thought no one understood what I was going through. I surrounded myself with other drunks like me. It was in this world that I was dying, wrapped in a chemical sense of comfort. These fellow drunks didn't judge me. They liked who I was, even though I hated who I was. I needed them, and they needed me. Still, I was miserable, embarrassed, and scared. I didn't realize until much later that they were lost too. Cloaking myself in a mask of normalcy, I hid my suffering and eased the pain with more alcohol. With all of that spinning around my brain in a tornado of confusion, I did the only thing I knew how to do. I did the only thing I thought made me feel normal and content: I drank.

One fateful day, I hit bottom. This wasn't the first but it was the worst yet. I looked in the mirror and hated what I saw. I had to make a choice. I could continue to drink, and die, or stop drinking and live. I could try to climb out of the abyss to an uncertain fate, or accept my current fate and drink myself to death. I could numb myself and await death, or throw away everything I knew and expose myself to the world and walk toward a place I wasn't sure existed. That day I decided I had to somehow, some way, try to quit drinking.

This is my story. A story of a drunk who decided to quit drinking. I am not special or unique. I am your brother, father, cousin, or co-worker. I exist in every family, race, creed, and social status. I'm not famous, nor do I wish to be. I am just a drunk who found a way to stop drinking. This is my journey, both physical and spiritual, to the world of sobriety.

Am I Like Brett Favre?

Could I be the Brett Favre of drinking? In the twilight of Brett Favre's football career, he would stand in front of a podium, holding back the tears, declaring that he was retiring. Then, a few short months later, he would sign with another team and play another season. Then, he'd retire again, and then to everyone's shock and dismay, come back yet again. Sports experts, journalists, and people around the water cooler would wonder: Why he is doing this? They knew he never would be able to play at the same level again. Why could everyone see it except him? I think he just declared his fourth retirement as I am writing this. Everyone is waiting to see if he really means it.

I also have retired from my drinking career only to come out of retirement. I guess that like Brett, I missed the glory of my drinking career. I missed hanging out with my buddies at the pub. I missed being the center of attention. I longed for what I thought were the good times. I couldn't imagine my life post-drinking. I knew my drinking always resulted in problems, but I thought that this time, it would be different. I suspect I wanted to recapture my drinking Super Bowl that would never come.

Like Brett, I came out of retirement blazing, hoping to reclaim the glory of past days. In fact, in my case, I found a new bottom. Each bottom I hit was worse than the previous one. I hope I now realize that I never can recapture the long-gone time when drinking was fun, sociable, and did not hurt me or others. In fact, there were no glory days at all.

So, I am retired. I have put down the bottle. I do have fond thoughts of those days in the pub, talking sports and politics, singing, and pretending to be carefree. However, I remember more of the neglected responsibilities, wasted money, the drinking to avoid the shakes, the hiding of bottles to avoid shame or detection, puking and washing it down with the next drink, and not remembering what I had done the previous night. It was a personal hell that I do not want to experience again.

Ya know, the good times

Random Thoughts

Come on Guys, I only drank when?

When I have a good day at work; when I have a bad day at work.

When it rains or snows; hurricane parties are great!

Weddings, funerals, christenings; family is important.

Watching a ballgame; going to a ballgame; thinking about the ballgame.

When I'm bored; you have to stay active!

Before sex, during sex, after sex; it is all about the romance.

When something really good or bad happens to me, to you, or to anyone I know. I'm a caring person.

When I have a problem to solve; when you have a problem; when I solve a problem; when I want to avoid a problem; I am a problem solver!

When I'm upset; when you are upset with me. I must be a counselor too.

When I'm at the pub. Of course, it is important to support your local economy.

When I work around the house, when I don't want to work around the house, or when I'm supervising the wife working around the house. I'm husband of the year!

When I need to fall asleep. Remember, a good night's sleep is important to good health.

When I need to avoid a hangover. I must have doctor skills.

When didn't I drink??

Maintenance Drinking

Late in my drinking career I found it absolutely necessary to maintenance drink during the day. It started innocently many years before on Saturday mornings after a hard night of drinking and partying. The gang and I would have a morning Bloody Mary, beer, or shot to clear up the fog. Sitting around our fraternity living room in the same clothes we wore last night, we would talk about the night of drinking we just completed like we won a battle in a war. The morning drink was no big deal. It even had a name, "hair of the dog that bit you." If it had a cool name it must be okay! Hey, we had a keg party planned that afternoon and another party that evening. It was our duty to be ready.

For years it was normal to get drunk every night and get and stay drunk all weekend. It was simply what we did and it was normal for our band of merry drinkers. It wasn't a problem; I got up and went to work every day and functioned fine. Yeah, sometimes I would be a bit hung-over, but who hasn't shown up for work with a hangover? One day, many years into my drinking career, I noticed in the afternoon I had a real craving for a drink. I felt different, not on top of my game. All I could think about was quitting time and getting to the pub to have that drink. That was okay, I work hard and I deserve it. When I got to the pub and had that first drink, everything was fine. All I needed was a drink to calm my nerves. As the weeks went on, the feeling at work would intensify and my left hand would start to shake. No problem, I'll just have a drink in the morning before work and all would be fine. All was fine, at least for a short while.

Before the decision to take the pre-work morning drink, my drinking week went pretty much like this: I would get up on Monday morning, get dressed and go to the office just like any normal person. I would supervise my employees, go to meetings and be the consummate professional. At four o'clock I would leave work and head straight for the bar. I would throw down four or five double Jack and Cokes throw some darts and do a few shots. At six o'clock, I would say my goodbyes and head home. On the way home I would pick up a fifth of Jack Daniels, which I would drink throughout the night until I ran out or passed out. This usually would happen between midnight and one AM. Tuesday through Thursday the pattern would be the same. However on Friday night, I would stay at the pub until about eight PM and drink twice as much. On the way home, I would stop and get a gallon of Jack for the weekend. That night I would drink until I passed out. On Saturday morning I would wake up and have a morning shot to get me going. I would nip at the bottle while I poked around the house or ran errands until the bar opened back up at noon. I spent the rest of my Saturday at the bar drinking and socializing until about seven or eight PM and then went home to work on the gallon until I lost consciousness. On Sunday I was up again with a morning shot and back at the bar at when they opened at two PM. At seven PM, I would leave the bar, walk out to my truck, change into my dart team tee-shirt and play on the dart league until about midnight. After the dart tournament ended, I would drive my drunken ass home and finish what was left in the bottle. I would come to Monday morning and start the cycle again. I actually thought my life was normal.

Based on the success of my weekend drinking, the decision to take the morning drink to get through the day seemed logical to me. The problem was I generally finished everything I had by the end of the night. My plan was simple; when I was relaxing on the couch in the evenings, I would wait until my wife was out of room and pour about two shots in a juice glass and hide it in the cabinet. In the morning, I would get up and get my morning fix. There is one important note about the morning shot. Although my body craved it, my stomach disagreed. In the morning when I choked down the morning shot my stomach often would decide to reject the offering and send it back in a most violent manner. Since this was all I had at the moment, I had no choice but to throw up back into the juice glass and then drink it back down. You would think that having to resort to drinking your own puke would be enough to think about quitting.

To my amazement, after only a few weeks of morning shots, the afternoon shakes came back. They scared the hell out of me. It wasn't a concern over my health or that my drinking had become a problem. It was the fear of someone noticing that I drink a lot. *This certainly will not do! I cannot be seen shaking at work. That is not what professionals do. No problem, a drink at lunch will hold me over.* The issue of where to get the lunch drink presented a problem. Having only a half hour lunch, a daily trip to a local watering hole was out of the question. I solved this dilemma by picking up a pint of rock gut whiskey with my nightly Fifth of Jack. I just hid it under the seat of my car and snuck out at lunch and drank half of it. When I got off work in the afternoon and made my daily trek to the pub, I would manage to kill the rest of the pint. The morning and lunch drink solved the problem. I wasn't drunk at work or anything; I just needed to have a drink to settle my nerves. Everything was back to normal. Then it happened. The times between the morning shot and lunch and the lunch shot and quitting time were too far apart. The shakes would start at ten AM and again at three PM. *What the hell is going on here?* I needed to fix this annoying problem. So, I engaged my finely pickled alcoholic brain for a classic alcoholic solution.

The solution required some detailed planning but as long as it solved the problem it was worth the effort. *I still take my shot in the AM and a drink at lunch. I'll just sneak in to work a couple of airplane size bottles of whiskey in my lunch sack for my now needed ten AM and three PM drink.* So, every night I would walk into the liquor store and buy a fifth of Jack Daniels, a pint of Evan Williams whiskey, and four airplane bottles of Wild Turkey. That liquor store clerk must have thought I was crazy. Many of my fellow recovering alcoholics would tell me they would go to different liquor stores to avoid the embarrassment. I frankly didn't care. The problem of how to take the ten AM and three PM shots without detection was overcome by a trip to the stall in the bathroom. *Oh, toothpaste, toothbrush, extra cologne and mouthwash were necessary because some people might get the wrong idea and smell the booze on my breath and think I have a problem. Which of course, I most certainly do not have a drinking problem.* Another problem solved. *What about the pain on my right side? Isn't that where the liver is? Could I be doing permanent damage to my body? It really worried me. No sweat, a drink makes that pain and worry go away too. Should I worry about shaking? Not really, as long as I sneak some maintenance shots during the day, once I got to the bar and had that first drink, that problem was solved too. As long as I am prepared twenty four hours a day to have that drink available if I need it, I will be OK. Sure it is a lot of work and requires a lot of detailed planning, but ya gotta do what ya gotta do, right?* One day I forgot to bring my little bottles. The result was a shaking seizure which landed me in the hospital. I thought my goose was cooked. I would be declared an alcoholic. My life would come crashing down around me. The doctor gave me what I thought at the time was a lucky misdiagnosis of Hypoglycemia. That was great because it gave me an excuse for looking or feeling bad at work. Someone would say "Hey Frank, do you feel alright?" My new response was, "that damn hypoglycemia is flaring up again." Another problem solved! What an incredible stroke of luck. I dusted myself off, left the hospital and headed directly to the bar. "Drinks are on me boys!"

OH, yea, I had things totally under control

Random Thoughts

What Someone Early in Recovery Sees

I woke up and got ready for work. I made my daily commitment not to drink and said "Just for Today."

Grabbed the trash on the way out the door and saw the wine bottles my love drank this weekend.

Put it out of my mind.

Got in the car and headed to work.

Turned off the radio when I heard a beer commercial.

Drove past Sue's Corner Pub; open, with a few familiar cars in the lot.

Bit my tongue and drove on.

Passed the liquor store I used to frequent daily.

I said "Just for Today."

Got on the highway and notice a pretty girl on a billboard.

Oh, it is a Jack Daniels AD. UGGH!

Checked my e-mail at work and got a retirement party flyer with pictures of people partying.

Started thinking of my excuse.

Overheard Jim bragging about how tore up he got last night at the bar.

Got my coffee and walked away.

Susan and Ken invited me to the local pub for the traditional two drink lunch.

Politely refused.

Looked out the window and observed the COORS truck driving by.

Smiled and went back to my desk.

Got invited for an after work drink.

Stated I don't drink.

Told to just have one.

Politely declined.

Drove home seeing all the signs and old haunts I used to visit.

Clutched my thirty day coin and said it is not worth it.

Got home and turned on the game I had been waiting to see all day. Counted twenty alcohol commercials during the game. But, they did say drink responsibly in every commercial.

That doesn't apply to this drunk.

Made a hotdog and craved a beer to go along with it.

Grabbed a Pepsi instead.

Took the dog for a walk and ran into the neighbors sitting in the garage drinking beer. Chatted and moved on.

Went to the eight PM meeting, talked about it and felt better.

Fell asleep sober for yet another day.

The GIG is Up

It was a normal day at work. Everyone was going about the business of the day. I remember I took a good maintenance drink in the morning. However, I did not have anything stashed at work that day. I was annoyed but not concerned. About ten AM, I started shaking worse than I ever shook before. I ate some candy

> *I read the News today.......*
>
> *Father Charged with Murder*
>
> *He was arrested on charges of murder and driving under the influence and failure to use a child restraint in a vehicle. The child, age two, died of massive head trauma*

to try to arrest it but it was to no avail. I remembered my last big attack of tremors which was misdiagnosed as Hypoglycemia and knew I was definitely in trouble. I shut the door to my office, closed my eyes and tried to ride it out. The shakes moved from my hands to my legs. My mouth quivered so much I could barely talk. The fear began to rise from the depths of my being. I wondered if I should sneak out and call out sick or maybe take a quick trip to the liquor store to get my fix. But I was paralyzed in place and I couldn't think straight. Finally a visitor noticed me and alerted my wife who worked on a different floor. Something was wrong with Frank, so Frank took another trip to the hospital. People generally walk into the emergency room and have to stand in a line to sign in and justify why they are there and then have to sit with dozens of sick people for hours waiting to be seen. When I walked into the emergency room my legs were so shaky and I looked so bad that the nurse jumped up from behind the desk and quickly put me into a wheelchair. I could barely talk or move. I was dying. I was immediately taken to a room where I was given an IV. A nurse

16

finally asked me the questions. "How much do you drink? Are you an alcoholic?" There was no hiding, lying or denying. I just didn't have the energy to lie. I responded in a quivering voice. "Yes I believe I am." This time the diagnosis was correct. I was suffering from the Delirium Tremors' (DT's). I was the typical drunk they had all too often seen. A pathetic man who was no different than the drunks down on skid row. What was more pathetic was that I was dressed like a respectable business man. At that moment I was not the successful professional, father, and husband I pretended to be. I was a drunk. It was embarrassing but no real surprise or shock to me. In some strange way I was relieved. I had been exhaustively hiding my drinking for so long and it felt good to tell another person I was sick. The doctor asked if she could talk to me in front of my wife. I said yes because she also needed to know the secret I had been hiding for so long. The doctor stabilized me and gave me a firm lecture on my off the chart liver enzymes and how I was killing myself. She was not empathetic or kind. She chewed my ass. She told me I would soon die if I didn't stop drinking.

I was released and she sent me home with some pills to ease the withdrawals that were sure to hit hard if I did decide to stop drinking. I promised myself that I would quit for good. I really meant it. I knew I was dying. I knew however I had the self-discipline to stop killing myself. I took the rest of the week off stating my Hypoglycemia flared up and withdrew with the pills. I was determined to stay clean. I was confident. That weekend I went to my first Alcoholics Anonymous meeting. This was a bump in the road and knew I could fix the problem.

I was cured ----NOT!

Random Thoughts

The Catch Phrase

People in meetings say this before they speak or share:

"Hi, I'm "BLANK" and I'm an Alcoholic."

This is the universally accepted way to introduce yourself in a meeting. It is also very effective for the newcomer who is unsure of himself and the others in this meeting. However, some people create their own catch phrases. Here are a few I have heard.

Hi I'm "BLANK' and by the grace of God and Alcoholics Anonymous I have not found it necessary to take a drink today. For that I am truly grateful.

Hi I'm "BLANK" and I am still an Alcoholic.

Hi I'm "BLANK" and I am a grateful recovering Alcoholic.

Hi I'm "BLANK" and I am a grateful recovered Alcoholic.

Hi, I'm "BLANK" and I am addicted to anything that makes me feel good.

Hi, I'm "BLANK" and I'm just here to listen.

Hi, I'm definitely an alcoholic and my name is "BLANK"

Hi, I'm an alcoholic and my problem is "BLANK'

After one gentleman would speak, he would say: *I don't know if what I just said helped you, but it certainly helped me.*

I'm thinking about this for my catch phrase:

Hi, I'm Frank and I'm a drunk in remission.

The Dry Drunk

I really wanted to quit drinking and I did. I declared myself sober and went to meetings. I was strong. *I am a former Army Officer with what I think is an important government job. I have been successful my entire life. I have conquered every challenge. I am respected in my community. I can and will do this!* What I didn't realize was that I wasn't truly sober. I just wasn't drinking. What I realize now is that I was what we

I read the News today.......
Drunk Man Dies after Trying to Slap Passing Train
Authorities say alcohol was involved in a man's deadly decision to try to "slap" a passing train. 23-year old was killed around 2 a.m. Thursday after being sucked under the train. He had been drinking at a bar to celebrate his birthday.

alcoholics refer to as a "dry drunk." I was in a new type of hell and I was miserable. I had to fight with every ounce of my being the overwhelming desire to drink. It overwhelmed my every thought. I could not stop myself from thinking about drinking. It was like an insect crawling around in my brain gnawing at my sanity. I was not a mean drunk. Although when I did get angry it was enhanced by my drinking. As a dry drunk I was a mean asshole. Everyone annoyed me. My wife later told me that she preferred me drunk than a miserable dry drunk.

The meetings did help keep me from drinking. I enjoyed sharing my experience and did feel some comfort that I was not alone in this struggle. But that is where it stopped. I was not ready to declare myself totally powerless when it comes to alcohol. I still thought that one day I could successfully drink again like normal people. They suggested things I didn't think I needed. They talked about working something called the 12 steps, and adopting a higher power. They told me I needed to get a sponsor. They told me I had to completely change my life and stay away from the people, places, and things that were center stage in my drinking career. I was supposed to be humble and admit I was powerless over alcohol. They seemed nuts to me! *I don't need all that. I'm not like them. I am strong. A couple of meetings a week and some will power and I'll be just fine.* All I needed to change in my life was not to drink. I still went to the pub every day and hung out with my buddies. I shot darts, laughed, joked and drank Sprite. I had this thing licked. I was going to do this it my way.

These people who were suggesting a way to beat this disease were a little too over the top for me. I thought they were absolutely crazy and had no idea what they were talking about. A common warning that I ignored was the saying; "If you go to the barbershop every day, you will eventually get a haircut." The barbershop was a reference for the bar or the haunts I frequented when I was drinking. I considered that saying something that was only meant for the weak ones. I was different. I was strong. I could go to the pub every day and not drink alcohol. *Why should I give up my friends and favorite activities? I should be able to live my way, on my terms.* I realize now that this was alcoholic thinking flowing through my brain even when I was not drinking. My illness was still in control. I couldn't have been more wrong and I was about to find out how wrong I was.

When I got my thirty day Sobriety card, I was proud of myself. I remained sober for thirty days and was cocky about it. Humility was not yet a part of my vocabulary. I have heard many definitions for humility, but this one I hang on my cubicle wall. "Humility is not thinking less of yourself, but thinking of yourself less." I was feeling healthy, energetic; the pain in my side (liver) was gone. I licked this thing my way and on my terms. What was strange was, if I wasn't happy before, I certainly wasn't happy now. I was nervous, restless, irritable, discontent, and just plain miserable all the time. I went from the frying pan into the fire. I replaced one type of hell with another hell. I thought about drinking twenty four seven. Every moment was a struggle. There was a civil war going on in my brain and I was losing. You see, alcohol at least gave me the chemical feeling of a fake peace and comfort. Being a dry drunk gave me nothing. There was a hole in my life. The answer was right in front of me. All I had to do was open my mind and listen to those people who were willing to help me. But my mind was closed, I was still thinking with an alcoholic brain and I couldn't see that a solution was being handed to me free of charge. I was blind, stupid, and ignorant.

I wouldn't open my mind and just listen to my fellow drunks that had the answer. On my forty seventh day of sobriety, I relapsed. It happened in the pub. Remember the barbershop quote? I did sit down in the barbershop chair and got a haircut. I didn't slip and fall into the whiskey. I chose to pick it up and drink it. I told myself I could handle it; this time it was going to be different. I learned my lesson. I learned how to control this thing. *I can now drink responsibly.* Despite all I was telling myself, I was about to find a new bottom and a new trip to hell.

Random Thoughts

Am I OK Today?

I am an alcoholic, I wake up every day and
tell my higher power thy will be done.

I hope that is OK.

I tried to stay sober, failed, and am trying again.

Is that OK?

I am a drunk who deeply desires never to drink again.

Am I OK?

I go to meetings every day and confide with my fellows.

Are they OK with me?

I seek my higher power every day and am
not sure when I truly will find him.

Is he OK with that?

I regret my past and try to do better each day.

Can the world be OK with that?

Despite my sins of the past, I am finding
serenity in my daily works.

Can I be OK with that?

I am selfish about my sobriety; yet try to
be selfless in all other affairs.

I think I may be becoming OK.

I went bed sober tonight.

I know that's OK!

The Relapse

It was a going away party for my wife and me at the pub. We were being transferred to Kentucky. This was normal for an Army family. All our best drinking buddies that were a part of our life for the past six years wanted to bid us a fond farewell. These were the people I saw every day. We played in the dart league together. We went to

I read the News today.......

Woman crashes into fire station, arrested for DUI.

A woman who crashed her SUV into a fire station on Monday night while her teenage daughter was in the car has been arrested for driving under the influence and child endangerment, a police sergeant said.

each other's houses on the weekends. When my wife was deployed to the war on terror and was in IRAQ, Kuwait, and Afghanistan for a year, the bar donated twenty five cents of all Sunday sales to us so that I could send her monthly care packages. These people were a huge part of our life.

Of course I could have a few drinks. It would be rude not to. How could I turn down that farewell shot? *I have been sober forty seven days. I learned my lesson and can now control my drinking.* I told myself I would not go back to my old ways. *I can drink tonight and not drink tomorrow.* So, I bellied up to the bar and ordered a whiskey and drank it down. All was immediately fine. The whiskey awakened me. That familiar feeling came back. The dry drunk got his relief. It was a great party. Things were back to normal. The plan was to have just a few. What happened was I had quite a few more than a few and despite my pledge to control it that night, all thoughts of control were gone after the first drink. When I got home I had a few more. I believed I deserved it and I could now handle it. I was convinced that I would be fine the next day. I told myself that I would not let this get out of control again. Well, one week later when the movers were picking up our furniture, I was the guy passed out on the dining room floor at eleven AM. The cycle has begun yet again. I was a hopeless drunk. We went to Kentucky and I went back to work. It didn't take long before I had to drink at work again to get through the day. I drank a fifth of whiskey every night and a good shot in the morning and the maintenance drinking at work soon followed. The weekends were beyond a blur. The old pain came back. I lived to drink and drank to live. I always had plenty of alcohol stashed all over the house, at work, in the car, and probably in places I still haven't found today. I was quickly killing myself all over again. Within weeks I was worse off than I was before I quit the first time. Those crazy people who warned me about going to the pub also told me that every bottom has a trap door and they were absolutely right and I fell headfirst through that trap door and was heading towards the last and final bottom. That bottom is death. It turned out that the only person that was crazy and didn't know the score in those meetings was me. The binge lasted about three months and I can honestly say I didn't have a sober moment. I knew it was a matter time before I would get fired, get arrested, or die. I honestly don't remember much of those three months. I still to this day ask my wife questions about things we did. It was so bad I didn't remember that one of my children came to visit for a week during that period. I lived in a three month semi-functional blackout. How I didn't get arrested, fired, or hurt someone or myself is a miracle. At that point I figured I had a few months to live and I didn't know how to get out of this mess. So I did what I did what I did best, I continued to drink.

HAPPY DAYS ARE HERE AGAIN?

Random Thoughts

Things "I think" I heard other recovering drunks say

There is nothing worse than a head full of AA and a belly full of beer.

People don't fall off the wagon, they intentionally jump!

It works if you work it and you die if you don't.

If you go to the barbershop every day, you will eventually get a haircut.

Keep coming back.

Insanity is doing the same thing over and over again and expecting different results.

One day at a time

I know I have one more drunk in me, but I'm not sure I have another recovery.

Every bottom has a trap door.

Live and Let Live.

You can't hear until you can hear and you can't see until you can see.

Holding resentment is like drinking poison and expecting the person you resent to die

Frank K

When I die, I don't know with any certainty where I am going, but it can't be that bad because I have already been to hell.

I'm allergic to alcohol; when I drink I break out in handcuffs.

I'm allergic to alcohol; when I drink I break out as an asshole.

I'm allergic to alcohol; when I drink I break out in Mike Tyson.

I want to die with dignity; Sober!

If I don't drink today, I won't get drunk.

I didn't get in trouble every time I drank, but every time I got in trouble, I was drinking.

There is nothing worse than a head full of AA and a loved one who is suffering.

The biggest pay raise I ever got was the day I quit drinking.

You know you're ready when the pain to stay the same is greater than the pain to change.

I have earned my seat at this table.

To keep it, you have to give it away.

All of us got here because our ass was on fire.

My brain is like a bad neighborhood, I don't want to go in there alone.

The Decision

I was at work in Kentucky, sitting in a toilet stall drinking my mid-morning airplane bottle of Wild Turkey. That pathetic maintenance drink to get me through the morning until I could get that lunch drink. I felt sick, disgusted, hopeless, dirty, and a failure. I was simply mentally, physically, and emotionally exhausted. *Here I am at work wearing nice shoes, a dress shirt a tie and hiding in the toilet*

I read the News today.......

South Dakota Man Arrested for DUI on Lawnmower

The 51 year old was arrested after filling up with gas and allegedly buying a beer.

The sheriff's deputy arrested him on charges of driving under the influence, having an open container of alcohol and littering for allegedly throwing the can in a ditch.

drinking. I felt like I was dying and I think I wished for death. I was a slave to alcohol and I didn't call the shots or control anything. I felt like a fool. I was a broken man with a secret that was killing me both physically, spiritually, and emotionally. It was at that moment I realized I needed to get help right then or I would certainly die. I knew I couldn't stop on my own. I had tried before and it just didn't work. Any attempt to take time off and DETOX in secrecy would probably result in a seizure that would most certainly kill me. I had to go away somewhere and get professional help. Fear of death was fighting the fear of doing something about this problem and I was paralyzed in place. In a moment of clarity I decided I had to act right then or die. That moment of clarity saved my life. I called the employer assistance office at work and confirmed I could ask for help with no legal repercussions. I spoke to my wife that evening about my decision and she gave me her support. Of course the conversation was over drinks. She did not know how bad I was. She must have been shocked and confused. I guess love is truly blind. The next day I gathered my nerves and went to my boss and told him I needed a leave of absence to get help for my drinking problem. He of course took me to his boss to repeat the admission and plea for help. And then all of us were off to see the big boss for round three. Boy, I needed a drink after that experience. I remember saying that this was the most personally and professionally embarrassing thing I ever said to anyone. This was my latest bottom and I didn't care because I had to take drastic measures.

I knew I didn't have to give a specific reason for my leave of absence. Medical information is protected under the HIPPA Act. I could have gotten a doctor's note with no specific diagnosis.

I could have claimed a family emergency or taken a vacation. It was clear to me that it was time for all the lies to stop. Most importantly, I had to stop lying to myself. So I intentionally backed myself into a corner so that I would not back out. I knew my alcoholic brain would do everything it could to talk me out of this decision. I came clean knowing that all eyes would be on me upon my return to work, family, and the community. It certainly was a risk but I just didn't trust myself and thought this was the best way to go. I now had the support of my boss, my wife, and my job was waiting for me. It was now up to me. I put myself in a position where success was the only and final option. If I said I was scared or lonely, that would have been a huge understatement.

Random Thoughts

The Thirty Day Card

AA gives things to mark milestones of sobriety. In my first attempt with AA to get sober, the first group I went to presented a business card to mark your milestones. The most common memento appears to be a chip. I had mentioned earlier that my first trip to AA was an abject failure because I was still playing God and was going to stay sober my way on my terms. I did receive a thirty day sobriety card and then relapsed on the forty seventh day. I considered throwing the card away. For some reason I didn't. It just stayed in my wallet. I didn't want to look at it because what once represented success now represented a pathetic, self-righteous failure. I can stay sober forty seven days my way, on my terms and apparently not one day more. I am glad I kept the card. The card now represents what I can achieve on my own which is not much at all. I later wrote this statement on the card. *"Never forget what a closed minded attitude will get you. NOTHING!!"* So many people in successful recovery told me that you can't do it your way. They said, *"Your way got you into this mess. Your way will lead to relapse. Why don't you try it a way that has actually worked for others?"* Those bastards were right again!

Now that I have far eclipsed forty seven days by surrendering to alcohol; embracing a higher power of my understanding; going to meetings to listen, share and learn; working with my sponsor; working the twelve steps every day; and living a selfless life, I now know what I can achieve with the program and a little help from my friends. The Beatles song with the same name means so much more to me now. Hey, songs that have a new meaning sober? That could be my next Random Thought.

The Pub Life

Late in my drinking career the pub life engulfed my entire social network. It changed from some place to stop by on the weekend to a daily trek as common and normal as getting up and going to work. When the work day ended, my bride and I would stop at the pub on the way home. It was a way to shed the burden of the grind of the job. We became fast friends with the owners who happened to also tend bar. Like flies to crap, we also

I read the News today.......

One jailed, another hospitalized after bar fight.

A man remains in Jail after he allegedly assaulted another resident on Thursday night.

The man was charged with felonious assault with harm to the victim.

Another person was also arrested at that time but was later released, with no charges being filed.

It is still unclear why the two were fighting.

became friends with the other afternoon regulars. All were great people, who worked during the day and would stop for a drink after work. Many were couples like my wife and me. Some were single men or women. We all got along great. We got to know each other very well. We would talk about our kids, jobs, sports, politics, or just tell the funny joke we heard at work that day. It was a small neighborhood pub and in that pub we found our second family. The afternoon clientele generally averaged in age from thirty five to sixty years old. There was a juke box from which we played the music of our youth. We became close enough to kid and joke and the juke box was one method. If someone had a problem we would tease them and attempt to lighten their stress through music. One day one of our friends was going through a tough break up. He was clearly upset and we sprang into action. We spent the evening playing break up songs and singing them loudly throughout the bar. Everyone joined in and we laughed until we cried. When my wife was released from her long stay in the hospital due to her stroke, she was met with loud cheers and of course, Billy Squires, Stroke Me on the juke box. Get laid off; play songs, get arrested play jailhouse rock. It was quite an experience and it seemed normal and innocent.

Since the pub was small, it only had room for two dart boards. So naturally darts became the passion. Internal competition soon branched out to two to three traveling dart teams. There was keen competition and rivalry to get on one of the dart teams. My father taught me to play darts on an old WIDDY American dart board as a child and I quickly became the anchor of our team. There were dozens of pubs in our town and traveling to other pubs to play darts and drink became part of our life. Trophies and team photos started to show up on the walls and it really seemed like home. Everyone had a collection of pub t-shirts. You would think we all had stock in the place. We probably should have given all the money we spent there each week.

Without the regulars and daily patrons, the pub would have gone under quick. Yes, there were the once a week patrons, but the pub survived on a couple of dozen drunks like me that ensured we graced the place with our presence and our money each and every single day.

The pub quickly became a more a social club. Every other Tuesday or Wednesday (I can't remember which, I was drunk) we would have a pot luck dinner. If our kids needed to find any of the parents for a ride to soccer practice or get some money for something to eat, they would show up at the pub. Weekend barbeques and tailgate parties were common.

This core group of about twenty five to thirty people became a close knit family at the bar. It seemed normal. We would take turns having weekend parties. We would help each other move to a new house or move a couch. This group of drinking buddies would invite each other into their world of family weddings, funerals, and graduations. It was a bond built around alcohol. It was a bond built on a very shaky foundation.

Heavy drinkers and alcoholics were huddled together creating what they thought was normalcy, friendship, and community. Our routine was four thirty to five thirty then home. It soon became four thirty to six PM. We eventually settled on staying until seven PM. Two dart nights a week kept me out until midnight. The bar opened at two PM on Saturday and noon on Sunday and I soon found some seemingly important excuse to be there. Yes, there were owners, but our group believed and felt the place was ours. It was a community hang-out for a bunch of middle aged adults. Not everyone was an alcoholic, but many of us were. Even our oldest daughter and boyfriend became part of the group. It seemed absolutely ordinary and it certainly seemed fun.

I realize now that there was something very wrong with that lifestyle. It was a life style with alcohol as the main event, the main dish, and this common bond was a tightrope that was dangerous and tricky to walk. Everyone had hopes and dreams and many were stalled or lost at the pub. The only balance was our daily drinking. It was the absolute wrong place for me and I suspect many of my buddies to be also. I almost lost everything, to include my life while I was living the pub life. Now I belong to another club and have formed many of the same bonds. The only difference is this club is centered on sobriety and becoming a better person. I like this club better.

Random Thoughts

Willpower

Willpower is an overrated trait. That is this drunk's opinion and it is born from my unfortunate experience. If willpower was so strong then why do we have so many people addicted to alcohol, drugs, cigarettes, gambling, sex, and food? Why do so many people go in and out of REHAB facilities with very little long term success? Why does almost every person in the world know of at least one person struggling with an addiction in their family or circle of friends? If simply making the decision to not do something anymore was all humans needed to overcome an obsessive or compulsive behavior, then the world would be free of addiction. I have not met a person who is addicted to something that was happy and content with the situation they have found themselves in. If they say they are, they are just lying and hiding their true misery. They are locked in fear. They are afraid to change. So, I'm going to put it out there. Willpower is not an effective tool to fight an addiction. This is not based on scientific fact as far as I know. This is my hard learned opinion. If you just like something, such as, watching sports on TV and decide you need to cut down because you have more important things to do, then willpower can work. However, if you have a mental obsession or addiction to watching sports then willpower alone simply will not work. I have come to absolutely, without a shadow of a doubt, believe that I am powerless over alcohol. That means I have no power or choice when it comes to drinking. Since I have no power and willpower comes from within me, then my willpower will have no effect when it comes to preventing me from taking that first drink. I know I need help from something or someone outside of myself to overcome my desire and mental obsession to take that first drink. I have tried willpower and have failed every time. There is no magic pill we can take to overcome alcoholism. But there are many ways an alcoholic can get help. Simply relying on the power that is within me is a recipe for disaster and the malady is truly an addiction.

I had to realize that the enemy is me and I could not win this life and death battle against myself. A twelve step program and belief in a power greater than myself, is what I use to stay sober. Each person has to find what works for them. If you are an alcoholic and think willpower is all you need then give it a try. One person with many more years of sobriety once said, if you think willpower can get you over your alcoholism then try this. Go to local grocery store and buy a box of chewable chocolate Ex-Lax. Proceed to eat the entire box in one sitting. Once you complete that, try to use your willpower to not go to the bathroom for twenty four hours. If you can do that, then you have the superhuman ability to quit drinking on willpower alone. Will power only suppresses an urge. Although suppressed, the urge is still there eating away at you. Telling you constantly you need what you are suppressing. You are in a miserable state of mind all the time. Eventually, I gave in to those powerful internal desires. To not drink, I had to change my way of thinking and treat the real problem; the desire or the mental obsession. The desire will always be with me. But now, because I chose to accept help, the desire is now a faint whisper not a loud roar.

Inpatient REHAB

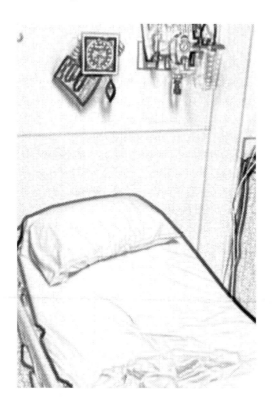

After revealing my problem to my boss, my wife, and most importantly me, it was time to go away and get help. I found out on a Thursday that my intake appointment was on a Friday at six PM. That gave me a day to think about what was about to happen. *I am a forty seven year old man and I am leaving my work, my family, my life and locking myself into the institution.* My biggest fear was the withdrawals. I had visions from old black and white movies of being strapped down in a strait jacket for my own protection as I go through violent and painful seizures. So of course, I drank over it. I drank heavily all day Friday and stopped for dinner at a Hooters across the street from the REHAB facility for a meal, a few Long Island Ice Teas, and a couple of shots of Jack Daniels. I have since learned that this type of drinking prior to heading to a REHAB center is very common and my wife held her tongue and did not object to my absolutely insane binge drinking. While I was sitting in the waiting room I apparently begged my wife to get me a small bottle for one last drink. She told me I didn't react very kindly to her refusal of my request. In fact she said I was an ass. I of course don't remember the exchange because I was beside myself with anxiety and fear. Oh, I think I was pretty plastered also.

Upon intake they asked me the last time I drank and I was brutally honest. They were not surprised and gave me a breathalyzer. My blood alcohol was .16. Anything over two would have landed me a night in the hospital for a more supervised DETOX. I kissed my wife goodbye and behind the locked doors I went. Other than the strip search they left me in my room for the evening. If it had been a normal night of drinking I would have had my last drink of the day at midnight and my first drink at six AM and if I got up to pee in the middle of the night, I would have had a shot. This night the drinking stopped at five thirty PM and the hell started at four thirty AM. The withdrawals hit hard. All I remember was lying on the floor of the bathroom puking and shaking from head to toe. I thought I was going to die. I was hot, cold, clammy, and thought I was coming out of my skin. The strength to stand was gone and had to crawl to the bed to lie down. It took what seemed an hour to pull myself into the bed to lie under the covers suffering. My mind was racing and I couldn't think straight. Yes, this was withdrawals! When breakfast came, the thought of eating was nauseating. I passed on the meal. The seconds miserably passed as I lay in bed trying not to shake. I wanted to walk out of there and find the nearest bar. The only reason I couldn't was I was too sick to move. Finally, around nine AM I got to see the doctor. He saw a pathetic drunk shaking from head to toe. I remember he asked me to hold my arms out at my side and my arms shook like a hummingbirds wings. He mercifully started me on medication to ease the withdrawals. The medicine helped and I slowly began to physically feel better. It took about three days to withdraw and on the fourth day I felt good enough and decided to refuse the medication.

Because I am a veteran with possible Post Traumatic Stress Disorder (PTSD) and a current Department of Defense employee, the doctors decided to put me in the military ward. At that time military wards were growing all over the country due to the effects of the wars in Iraq and Afghanistan. These Soldiers were suffering from everything from addiction to pain killers, drugs, and alcohol to severe emotional trauma. All this was fueled by Post Traumatic Stress from their wartime experience. PTSD is no joke and it is a devastating reality for an entire generation. These Soldiers need every dollar of research and assistance possible. Being older, I took on the role as a friendly ear to those great patriots. I was comfortable in this group. We shared a common bond.

I spent ten days in the facility and a lot of it is a blur. The effects of withdrawals made my memory of the time very foggy. Now I understand that true recovery doesn't begin until after withdrawals have ended. I do remember I attended classes and ate like there was no tomorrow. The year prior to this point I had lost forty pounds because I rarely ate and drank my meals. People used to tell me I looked good. They would ask me if I was losing weight. I knew I was just plain sick and dying of malnutrition. The education in the facility was pretty good but not great. I did learn some techniques for staying sober.

I did get a chance to share my troubles and listen to others. We did YOGA one day and that was very interesting and relaxing. We did gym time every day and I judged my physical recovery by the ability to shoot a basketball. The first week I was so weak I couldn't reach the basket from ten feet. By day ten I had the strength to make some baskets. I was now physically withdrawn from the booze and feeling good. My mind was starting to clear. I was able to reflect on my life and where drinking had landed me. I knew I couldn't stay away from work forever, so I talked myself out of there and into an outpatient facility. It is amazing how easy it is to get into REHAB and how hard it is to get released. Oh, you can walk out anytime, but to be declared ready to leave is a different story. In my case, I made a compelling argument that in my case a transition from inpatient to outpatient, then back to the work world was best for me.

On the tenth day I walked out of the rehabilitation center with some hope and a new fear. You see it is easy to not drink when you are locked in a hospital. It is a little different when you are free. Alcohol would be available twenty four seven again. One slip or one moment of weakness or frustration could propel me into another drinking binge. I knew that I had to change every part of my life to win this battle but I just didn't know how. I would soon learn how in outpatient REHAB.

I was scheduled to report to an outpatient facility the next day. The first night at home was fine. There were no major cravings. I was cautiously optimistic. Little did I know, my life was about to change.

Random Thoughts

Songs that have new meaning
since becoming Sober

Music has always been a great love of mine; I have enjoyed everything from Rock to Classical and everything in between. Prior to getting sober, there were only a handful of songs in which the lyrics really moved me. Now music has come alive in a manner that is inspirational. Certain songs that I have listened to my entire life suddenly have great meaning and I can relate them to my struggle and journey.

(This list will never be complete)

Bruce Springsteen and the E-Street Band - Lost in the Flood

The Beatles – A Little Help From My Friends

Kenny Chesney – That's Why I'm Here

P.O.D. - Alive

Neil Young – The Needle and the Damage Done

The Beatles – Let it Be

Pink Floyd – Comfortably Numb

Lou Reed – Underneath the Bottle

Pink Floyd – Dark Side of the Moon Album – (Except the Song "Money")

Frank K

Blind Faith - Can't Find My Way Home

Eagles - Hotel California

Bruce Springsteen – One Trick Pony

The Who – Won't get Fooled Again

Rare Earth - I Just Want to Celebrate

Neil Diamond – I Am, I Said

Gary Wright – Dream Weaver

Cat Stevens – Drywood

Six Am – All their music

Outpatient REHAB

I arrived at the outpatient REHAB facility and endured the fun strip search. Since I was coming and going daily, this would be part of my morning routine. The search usually was conducted by two females because there were no males working the morning shift. This could normally embarrass some men. In my case, I was the first one to strip and go skinny dipping at one of my parties, so it was no big deal. Truthfully, I was beginning to learn a little humility. This REHAB facility taught a program called Recovery Dynamics. Six hours of daily education based upon the principles of Alcoholics Anonymous. This was no joke. They didn't want to hear your story. They already knew your story. They gave you classroom instruction about the disease of Alcoholism and addiction. They taught the twelve steps and gave hours of homework each night in the form of tests and writing assignments. It was overwhelming to many and those that hadn't accepted that they were truly sick stood out in the group. Here is where the light bulb came on in my mind. This is where I learned I had a disease of the body and the mind. I finally realized and admitted I was powerless over alcohol and

> *I read the News today......*
>
> *Every fifth Russian man*
> *dies of Alcohol*
>
> *The Russians drink an average of 15.76 liters of pure alcohol every year, which makes them the fourth most drinking country in the world. By far the highest proportion of alcohol-attributable mortality is in the Russian Federation and neighboring countries, where every fifth death among men and 6% of deaths among women are attributable to the harmful use of alcohol.*

my life had become unmanageable. I learned I had to stop playing God, and turn this problem over to my higher power, whatever or whoever that may be. I was awakened. I was like a sponge. I sucked up knowledge and craved it like I craved alcohol. I stayed in the program for three weeks and would not leave until I completed step four. Here is where I finally understood that I had an incurable but treatable disease. A person with type 1 diabetes must take insulin every day and restrict certain foods from their diet or they will die. It is the same for alcoholics; they must completely abstain from alcohol and take daily treatment. That treatment is through meetings, meditation or prayer, reading literature, work with a sponsor, and working and living the twelve steps every day. I had to be willing accept a power greater than myself. All this is necessary because this disease is a disease not only of the body, but also of the mind. A person can withdraw from alcohol in three 3 days to a week. If that was all that had to be done, there would be far fewer alcoholics in this world. However, the mental obsession to drink must also be controlled every day. That is what I learned in the outpatient REHAB. The instructors were also recovering alcoholics. Most of the nursing staff was in recovery also. Even the chief head shrink was in recovery. This is important, because they understood who we were and what we were going through. They could relate when we hurt and see through our whining crap. Upon my release, I was told to go directly to a meeting. I was warned if I didn't I would surely end up back in REHAB, in jail, or dead. I listened for the first time and went to a meeting that night.

Random Thoughts

You might be an Alcoholic

Did you ever get out of the shower and notice bruises on your body and had no clue where they came from? You might be an Alcoholic.

Did you ever talk to people about what you did last night and you have no clue what they are talking about? You might be an Alcoholic.

Have you ever used the closet as the toilet? You might be an Alcoholic.

Did you ever worry about running out of liquor? You might be an Alcoholic.

Did you ever see a scratch on your car and have no clue how it got there? You might be an Alcoholic.

Did you ever drive down the road with one eye shut so you see one car in front of you instead of three? You might be an Alcoholic.

Did you ever eat fast food at three AM? You might be an Alcoholic.

Does your plan for the weekend involve at least two drinking events? You might be an Alcoholic.

Do you find it appalling when someone says they have had enough after just two beers? You might be an Alcoholic.

Does having a drink make you feel better and not drinking make you feel like crap? You might be an Alcoholic.

Do you drink before a party so that you can have just a few to appear to drink normal at the party? You might be an Alcoholic.

If you always have alcohol in the house, you might be an Alcoholic.

Did you ever wake up and find late night ATM receipts and an empty wallet and wonder what you spent all that money on? You might be an alcoholic.

If you have to tell yourself you are not an alcoholic? You might be an Alcoholic.

Do people ask you to slow down or take it easy? You might be an Alcoholic.

Do you feel most comfortable and confident with a drink in your hand? You might be an Alcoholic.

Is an eye opener in the morning normal to you? You might be an Alcoholic.

Do you take back roads to avoid a DUI? You might be an Alcoholic.

Does the bartender know what drink you are going to order before you say a thing? You might be an Alcoholic.

What I Now Understand About the Disease

I am not a doctor and I am not offering anything but what I understand from personal experience about this incurable disease. This description is what happens in my mind and body and what ironically also happens in all the other drunks I know.

It is a disease that affects both the mind and the body. When an alcoholic takes that first drink of the day, something happens that doesn't happen in what we drunks call normal drinkers. A normal drinker can have one or two drinks and stop. We cannot drink in that manner. In fact, observing such behavior confuses the alcoholic. When an alcoholic drinks that first drink, he craves

> *I read the News today.......*
>
> *In the United Kingdom, the death rate from liver disease has risen 500% over the past 40 years. It is predicted that, within a decade, liver disease will overtake cardiovascular disease as the leading cause of death in the UK,*

another and another, and another. Thus the endless cycle begins. We are never full; we can't stop until we run out of alcohol, run out of time, run out of money, pass out, or find ourselves in handcuffs or in a coffin. The most unfortunate of our lot find an early grave. I remember sitting at the local pub and watching a normal drinker look at his watch and walk out leaving half a drink unfinished. I was shocked. I thought what a waste. *This is just stupid and wasteful.* This is another example of alcoholic thinking. That is the mind of an alcoholic at work. I could not understand normal drinkers. *How can they just take it or leave it?* I wondered what the hell was wrong with them. I never asked myself what was wrong with me. So, I would have another drink and forget about it.

I was also taught that an alcoholic does not metabolize alcohol as efficiently as the normal drinker, thus allowing him to drink more before the effects kick in. The bottom line is once we get going, our willpower cannot stop us. This has been referred to as a binge or spree. A drinking spree can last a night, a weekend, months, or years. My last spree lasted three months. I can honestly say that I had some level of alcohol in my blood stream for the entire time. When an alcoholic wakes up from a spree, whether he is in bed, on the floor, in jail, or has no clue where he is, he feels disgusted with himself. He has feelings of remorse, self-pity, anger, and guilt. He tells himself, I must stop. I can't do this anymore. I'll never do this again! He truly means it. He really wants to stop the insanity. Then depending on the alcoholic and how far gone he truly is something starts to happen. For some like me, it starts within hours, for some within days. It doesn't matter how long it takes, it happens the same for all of us. We start feeling, restless, irritable, uncomfortable, and discontent. The mental obsession kicks in and the only thought going through your mind is having a drink. This is the most insidious and evil part of the disease. Your mind will tell you to drink. Your mind will lie to you. My mind tells me something like this. *"Hey, look at yourself; you feel like crap, you're not happy. Hey, you were happy last night at the Pub. Just a have one drink and you will feel better. Just don't have a lot. Today will be different. You can control it. Just have one or two drinks and stop."* Well, it always made sense to me, I felt like crap and I thought I could surely control this thing this time. So, I took that first drink and it was like being shot out a cannon. Frank was off on another uncontrollable drinking spree.

The disease of the mind has done its job and has gotten us to pick up that first drink. Then it turns us over to the disease of physical craving; the disease of the body. So off we go again and again with no end in sight. It becomes an endless cycle. No willpower we can muster up can beat the mental obsession and craving. We want so desperately to stop; we really do, but just can't break the cycle. Even a week or a month locked in a REHAB facility will be fruitless because once we are out of the facility the mental obsession overcomes us again. Those normal people who don't understand the disease look at us with disgust and bewilderment. They tell us things like this: why don't you just stop; just slow down; you're killing yourself; how many jobs are you going to lose because of your drinking; don't you care about your family? The answer is we do care and we want so desperately to stop this endless cycle. We are in a personal hell and can't find our way out. We are in a civil war of the mind and are losing the battle every day. We are waiting to die. Many of us wish for death because we think it is the only way to end this self-inflicted personal hell we have found ourselves in.

No one can truly understand what an alcoholic feels except another alcoholic. When a normal person or figure of authority questions or lectures us on why we should not drink as we do, we simply can't explain it because they just don't understand the feeling and mindset of an alcoholic when he is separated from the drink. If they understood, they wouldn't be asking the questions or delivering the lectures. They have never experienced those feelings of restlessness, irritability, and discontent. These hopeless and frustrating feelings can only be relieved by a drink. We so desperately want non alcoholics to understand our disease, but we have come to just accept they never will and we wouldn't want them to pay the high price it costs to understand it.

Random Thoughts

My Friends

One major reason I delayed dealing with my alcoholism was my dearest friends. I would see them every day at the pub. We played in the dart league together. We discussed sports, politics, and share the events of the day with each other. They would buy me a drink and I in turn would buy them one. We rotate houses for weekend parties. This was my community. My community loved me. I needed them and they needed me.

What a crock of bull$%#$!

When I quit drinking, I was cast aside like an empty beer bottle. I was no more than a drinking buddy. I was someone to keep them company while they drank. They in retrospect were the same for me also. Since my sobriety, only one of my great friends has ever called me just to say hi. This was a great lesson to learn.

Now my dearest friends are my fellows. A fellow is a person you see at the meetings. We call our group a fellowship and here is where I found people who truly care about me. If I don't show up at this new club for a few days, they actually worry and give me a call or check in on me. My pub buddies have long replaced me and forgotten me and that is the best thing that could have ever happened to me.

I am grateful for my fellows and I don't regret losing my drinking buddies.

What was I Thinking?

Arguing with the Wife

My insistence to be right and my love for chaos made this drunk do some pretty immature and stupid stuff throughout my drinking career. How I handled a simple disagreement with my wife was a perfect example of alcoholic thinking. As with all couples, spats and arguments are a normal part of a relationship. People are individuals and will naturally disagree. However, my ego told me I had to win every argument at any cost. Add alcohol to the mix and you get Frank the drunken asshole.

I had this unwavering rule that we should never go to bed until an argument or dispute was settled. I believe a priest gave me that technique in a pre-marriage class prior to my first marriage. No matter how small the dispute was, I refused to go to bed until it was resolved in a manner that was acceptable to me. It didn't matter if we had the most important day of our lives planned in a few hours and needed our sleep, Frank was going to have all the attention and keep everyone up until he got his say and got his way.

This is how it would typically go down. After a good night of drinking, an argument would start. It would generally be about the kids or money. Amazingly it was never about my drinking. We would exchange opinions on a subject and it would escalate to an argument. My wife and I have the ability to say just the right thing to push each other's buttons. At one point in the argument she would decide she had said enough and would state she was tired, stop talking and go to bed. This incensed me to the core of my being. *We are in an argument. Someone has to win. I mean I need to win. How could she just end the argument with no resolution and just go to bed? This massive life changing issue needs to be resolved. So, I now the argument turned into "how dare you go to sleep?" "You obviously do not care about me."* She would of course pull the covers over her head and I would get mad and drink more. I would pace around the house and make noise to ensure she knew I was not happy with her. If that didn't work, I would go into the bedroom and continue to argue until I made her get up and settle the dispute. Oh, yeah, I was drinking the whole time and it was her fault. This would generally continue until I was so drunk, I passed out. That is the definition of an asshole in action or alcoholic drinking and thinking.

Now that I am sober, one thing has changed and one thing hasn't. We still disagree and occasionally argue over things, but now if we can't come to this agreement, we agree to disagree. If one of us is tired, we just put it off until the next day or generally just drop it all together. When I look back at the way I acted, I am truly embarrassed. I have apologized for my behavior and got a good belated earful about it too. This did annoy me but I guess I had it coming. We now can go to bed mad and wake up happy because I am no longer a drunken asshole.

There Isn't a Cure Yet but I Found a Treatment

I have described an incurable disease that not only affects the body but also effect the mind. No personal willpower, no encouragement from loved ones, no trips to jail, no loss of jobs, no bankruptcy, nothing can force the alcoholic to stop. So how could there be a solution? Well millions of alcoholics have found the solution and managed to live their lives sober. They live happy lives with serenity. They are productive members of this world we live in. Yes, and they are still alcoholics, just a happy sober version.

The solution I describe here is the one I found. I found it through the program of Alcoholic Anonymous. I am not saying that Alcoholics Anonymous is the only means to get sober. Nor am I a spokesperson for the program. I talk about it here because it is part of my journey to sobriety.

The solution is not complex. If you can overcome the mental obsession, you will not take that first drink. If you don't take that first drink, then you will not start the destructive cycle.

This is how I and many of my fellow alcoholics overcame the mental obsession daily. It has been best described to me as having a psychic change that fights the mental obsession. Think of a tool kit. Without the proper tools, we can't fix something that is in need of repair.

The first tool is our fellows. These are other recovering alcoholics that are living every day sober. They understand you, the alcoholic. They know where you have been. They feel what you feel. They know the way out. The easiest way to meet them and make them part of your life is Alcoholic Anonymous. Yes, you have to go to those meetings.

The second tool is a sponsor. This is a person who has used these tools to live a sober life. It is not a burden for them. Part of their continued sobriety is to help the newcomer. Going to meetings and getting a sponsor puts you right in the middle of a fellowship of people like you. They are alcoholics that have found the solution you have been seeking.

The third tool is to work the program daily by completing the 12 steps and live the steps daily. This may sound a daunting task but it is not. I Imagined the time I spent thinking about drinking, searching for the next drink, actually drinking, and dealing with the problems created from drinking. A little time each day is nothing compared to the time it takes to live an active alcoholic's life. How do we work it daily? Most recovering alcoholics with years of sobriety (yes, they do exist) will say you must complete the twelve steps and live them daily. It starts with complete surrender. This happens in the first step. Admitting that I am powerless over alcohol and my life has become unmanageable. Just completing the twelve steps is just the start. Most successful recovering alcoholics work them every day.

These are the original Twelve Steps as published by the book "Alcoholics Anonymous":

1. We admitted we were powerless over alcohol—that our lives had become unmanageable.
2. Came to believe that a Power greater than ourselves could restore us to sanity.
3. Made a decision to turn our will and our lives over to the care of God *as we understood Him.*
4. Made a searching and fearless moral inventory of ourselves.
5. Admitted to God, to ourselves, and to another human being the exact nature of our wrongs.
6. Were entirely ready to have God remove all these defects of character.
7. Humbly asked Him to remove our shortcomings.
8. Made a list of all persons we had harmed, and became willing to make amends to them all.
9. Made direct amends to such people wherever possible, except when to do so would injure them or others.
10. Continued to take personal inventory and when we were wrong promptly admitted it.
11. Sought through prayer and meditation to improve our conscious contact with God *as we understood Him*, praying only for knowledge of His will for us and the power to carry that out.
12. Having had a spiritual awakening as the result of these steps, we tried to carry this message to alcoholics, and to practice these principles in all our affairs.

Ok, you just read the list and saw a whole bunch of God in the list. Don't freak out!

I, like many other active Alcoholics, were turned off by the mention of God or a higher power. I did not need that higher power in my life. *Look how good I've done on my own. Oh, crap, my life is actually a mess. Maybe playing my own personal God did not work out very well after all. Maybe, this higher power thing is worth a shot.* The twelve steps have nothing to do with an organized religion. It does ask you to find a higher power of your understanding. It is more a spiritual program. Your higher could be God or the 12 steps itself. Many start by opening their minds to the possibility of a higher power. Your fellows don't care how you see your higher power. They are just happy to see you at the meeting trying to stay sober, "Just for Today." The journey through the steps is your own and all I can say is I am happy and sober because I stopped playing God, completely surrendered, worked the steps, and work the program daily. I have my life back. I have a good life. I have a higher power of my understanding that I choose to call God. I work the program every day and I know with most certainty, that if I stop working the program, I will drink again and die an Alcoholics death. That death is often slow, painful, and alone.

Thank you for sticking with this to this point. If you are not an alcoholic, hopefully you are starting to better understand this disease. If you are and want the life of a personal hell to end, give it a shot. If you are like I was, you may be about to lose everything anyway.

Random Thoughts

He knew the whole time!

During my drinking career I made it an art to hide the fact that I was drinking. Frequent showers, mouthwash, breath mints and cologne were a must, especially at work.

At the height of my drinking I shared an office with a man I respected very much. We would spend a great deal of time debating everything from the existence of God, science, politics, or whatever seemed news worthy. The conversations were intelligent and engaging. Oh yeah, I was also under the influence during most of these conversations. I looked forward to our daily verbal jousts. What I did not know was that he was keenly aware that I was struggling with a drinking problem. He never mentioned it or led me to believe he knew my dark secret. Even when he would arrive at work to find me sleeping one off in my chair, he said nothing. I would just tell him I was tired or I had a late night. It is amazing how slick and smart I thought I was. What I didn't realize was he was waiting for me to say something. He knew that any attempt to discuss the issue would just result in my excuses and lies. He also was keenly aware that any mention of my drinking would have resulted in me recoiling from him like a hot flame.

When I did finally admit that I might a have a small problem and probably needed to get things under control, he immediately began to talk to me. It was as if he had been waiting for a signal from me. I imagine he had to hold himself back many times waiting for the opportunity. This is a critical lesson I learned about dealing with others who suffer. No words or preaching can affect a sick person until they are willing to listen. If he had brought it up first, I would have recessed deeper into my own denial and shunned him as if he were the devil himself. He still checks up on me periodically. He understands me and cares.

More on Maintenance Drinking

IT WAS A TYPICAL DAY IN MY INSANE WORLD. The alarm went off and my beautiful bride rolled over and hit the snooze button as she always does. I spring out of bed with great purpose. I make a bee-line to the kitchen cabinet. On the top shelf strategically tucked out of sight is a four ounce glass of whiskey that I prepared the night before. I look to ensure the misses is still asleep and quickly down my morning medicine and am ready to start my day. I pack my lunch which I probably won't have the stomach to eat and ensure I hide two or three airplane bottle of whiskey in my lunch bag for work. Brush my teeth, lots of cologne and mouthwash and the wife and I head off to work.

The hours between seven thirty and ten AM go fine. This professional man is dutifully going about the business of the day. Around ten AM, that all too familiar feeling comes over me. The shakes start and the stomach feels funny. I can't concentrate and panic starts to set in. I quickly excuse myself to the bathroom, settle into a stall, and take a shot to settle my nerves. Take a quick rinse of mouthwash and back to work with no one the wiser. I repeat the ritual at noon and two PM to survive the day.

As quitting time comes, the feeling starts to come over me yet again. I count the minutes until I can walk out the door and head to the bar for some real drinks. Once in the car the wife announces we are going to the grocery store. Panic immediately pours over me. *How long is this going to take?*

Why is she telling me now? What is her problem? If I knew the night before, I would have brought an extra shot to hold me over. Just hold it together and don't let anyone see your hands shaking. Push the cart; it will help you steady your hands. Why is she taking so long? I'm not going to make it! Think quickly! Excuse yourself and tell her you will be right back. There is a liquor store across the street. Go there and get back before she is done shopping. I drive across the street and buy the biggest bottle. I get in the car and take a look for cops and passers buy and then take a solid drink. With the shakes subsided and the nervousness gone, I go back to the store to meet up with my bride. All is back to normal. I have enough liquor for tonight, tomorrow, and any excursion she may dream up for tomorrow.

The guilt, self-pity, anger, and demoralization that I felt that day were overwhelming. It wasn't so overwhelming to quit but it was when I realized I was in big trouble and something had to give. But I still wasn't ready. I continued to drink.

What was I Thinking?

Deported for the Night

I was stationed in Indianapolis, Indiana and was a Battalion Executive Officer for a small training Battalion of fifty experienced Infantry Soldiers. Our job was to travel about the country and train and evaluate National Guard Infantry units. It was gritty field duty with long hours and family separation. We loved every minute of it. The Soldiers in our unit were seasoned and experienced for the pre Iraq war timeframe. Since

I read the News today.......

Young man charged with DUI for boating accident; passenger still missing

A Massachusetts man has been accused of operating a boat while under the influence of alcohol.

The incident threw the DUI perpetrator, as well as a friend of his, overboard into the Marshfield Harbor on Saturday night. The second victim has yet to be located.

the Global War on Terror, our Soldiers today are much more proficient. They also have paid a large price for that experience as many of them find themselves struggling to fit in to the world after fighting a war. My group of Soldiers worked hard and played even harder. It was the largest group of hard drinkers I ever served with and the Battalion Commander and I led the pack in every way to include the heavy drinking. When in garrison, a Friday afternoon raid on the local strip club was the norm. The girls at the club were always glad to see us and some of the wives hated me for dragging their husbands to the club. In fact on one fateful Friday afternoon one of the wives walked into the club and demanded I take her to her husband. Of course, he was getting a lap dance and had his face buried in an ample serving of a D cup sandwich. You could say we stretched the Army values to their limit.

We did work hard and spent a lot of time on the road traveling to Army posts to run exercises. Our road trips were epic. One of our yearly treks was to Fort Drum, NY. As the Executive Officer, I was in charge of all logistics to include travel plans. The Army is very strict on how far you can drive in a day and I used that to our group's advantage. The trip to Fort Drum was a two day convoy of vans that just happened to stop us for the night at Niagara Falls, NY. The hotel I chose was five hundred yards from the walking bridge to Canada. I ensured we left at five AM on day one so we could arrive in Niagara, NY around noon. This gave us all day and night to rest for the remainder of the drive. Actually it gave us all day to drink, then when we were good and primed, we would walk across the bridge and assault Canada for the evening. We attacked their bars, their night life and of course their women. Many Canadian women woke up the next day in our hotel on the US side. This yearly plan went without a hitch the first two years but there was a small glitch the third year.

The third year we descended yet again upon Niagara Falls, and we encountered a small problem. The friendly hotel clerk, who got a kick out of us destroying the hotel once a year, told one of us about a bar on the US side where we might enjoy starting our adventure. We were sitting around the picnic tables slamming home toxic Long Island Ice Teas that some of the NCO's mixed up when we were told of the bar. About half of us decided to give it a go and the rest stayed at the hotel to get their drink on before crossing the border to Canada. Two van loads of already buzzed troops headed to the bar. We managed to get lost and ended up in a less desirable part of town. We did find a local pub and two of the guys went in to ask directions. The rest of us waited in the vans and pounded down our home made swill. A few minutes later I noticed our two buddies sprinting towards our vans with six angry patrons chasing them down the street with baseball bats. When fifteen of us piled out of the vans, the baseball bat wheeling locals quickly backed down. Well, sort of.

We got about a mile down the road and stopped at a gas station for directions when the entire Niagara Police Department blocked our vans in with four squad cars. There was even a cop on a bicycle. When they found out we were military, they wanted to talk to the senior officer. Of course that was me. I figured twenty four drunken Soldiers getting arrested within a mile of a national landmark and world treasure for drunk and disorderly, DUI, and inciting a riot might not look good on my record. I explained that we were heading to an important mission and just blowing off some steam. I reminded the officers that the Army will over react to this incident and my troops could lose their careers. I laid it on thick. The cops bought my not too big of an exaggeration and cut me this deal. We were to drive back to the hotel and park and lock the vans for the night. We were then instructed that all of us were to immediately walk across the bridge to Canada. We were to get whatever we needed to get out of our system outside of the United States. We were finally told to not return until dawn and get our butts out of their town first thing in the morning. We followed their orders like good Soldiers and invaded Canada for the night and had one hell of a good time.

This was a drinking story I often told at the pub receiving laughs and drunken accolades. The truth behind this story is if the police officer arrested us. The Army would have been embarrassed in the press and many a career and family would have been destroyed. All this because of alcohol fueled drunken leadership.

So, I think I can say I'm the only Army officer to get his unit deported from his own country. What was I thinking?

Character Defects

Every human being has character defects. Some of us are selfish. Many of us suffer from pride. Quite a few are suffocated by their fears. Greed drives people to do unthinkable acts. There are the liars, the thieves, and the terminally lazy. All people have character defects. The seven deadly sins are a good starting point to begin a self-evaluation but there are hundreds of defects to choose from. One of my big ones is that I have to be the center of attention. I have to be seen in the crowd. I have to lead every project and get all the credit and pats on the back due me. I can be extremely selfish.

Another defect is the comfort I feel swimming in chaos. When a normal person experiences or is confronted with chaos, they do everything they can, as fast as they can, to get out of it or to get away from it. This alcoholic lived, slept, ate, and swam in chaos. I wasn't alive or aware unless I was starting or jumping into a chaotic situation. Fights, conflicts, and debates made me feel alive. If there was no chaos, Frank would stir something up to get the party going. I knew how to push the buttons of everyone around me to get the attention I needed. Today I try to avoid chaos at all costs. It seems to make life less cluttered and complicated. Someone once said that they would rather be happy than right. So, now I can avoid chaos by letting someone else think they are right. If there is no conflict, there is no fight or bad feelings. This is working best with my wife. She thinks she is right and I am conflict free and happy. Living in chaos and always having to be right was just another branch of selfishness.

However, this character defect did bode me well in my quest to become and remain sober. I am very selfish about my sobriety. I guard it like a prized priceless jewel. But this form of selfishness is good and necessary if I am to live life in a selfless manner. That sounds a little crazy. Be selfish to become selfless.

Let me explain. I stated that all people have character defects. Some defects are out of control and some pop up occasionally. When I was an active alcoholic all my character defects were intensified and they were all fueled by my selfishness. Alcohol and the need to have it came first. It was the center of my universe. Everything else was put on hold until I had that right deadly chemical balance in my body. When I was comfortably drunk, I was ready to take on life. But, since I was drunk, I was not capable of handling life with any degree of true success. In fact, I am amazed I didn't do far more damage than I did. I guess it was dumb drunk luck. Whatever it was, alcohol was the king and I was the court jester. I had to take alcohol out of my life and body for good. I had to be selfish about that. I have spent a lot of time and effort tearing Frank apart and rebuilding a new Frank that is not a slave to alcohol.

In this selfish quest for self-improvement, I have freed myself to focus on what is important and it is not me. I try now to focus on my family, friends, coworkers, and fellow human beings. I no longer desire to be the center of my own personal universe, but instead want to be just a happy productive member of the world. The most important thing is I accept the fact that I have many character defects. They will always be in me. Now I try to replace them on a daily basis with better traits. I am not perfect and I will still occasionally catch myself acting out badly due to my character defects. The difference is I recognize it when they come out and stop the behavior before it gets out of control.

So, my selfishness about my sobriety makes me more selfless.

Random Thoughts

Should You Hire or Re-hire
A Recovering Alcoholic?

I say absolutely yes. Why wouldn't you want someone in your employ that will never be hung over or drunk at work? If the job involves driving company vehicles, you will never get that call that your employee has gotten into an accident, hurt someone and your employee was drunk. If that person calls in sick, they really are sick. They are not too drunk or hung over to come to work. You at least have one person perfectly clear headed at work the Monday after Super Bowl Sunday. This person will most likely be a team player and will put the needs of your company before their own. He will not take this opportunity for granted because he knows he have been given a second chance on life. This person is not trying to feed an addiction and will not steal to feed a habit. He will have a keen understanding of other employees suffering from any emotional issue and will jump in and help.

Now, you must realize that this person has an illness and could relapse. With all employees, changes in work patterns, attitude, and demeanor, may indicate that something may be going on in his or her life. These changes should be evident if you or your supervisors are paying attention. Every hire is a risk. A person in recovery is definitely worth the risk.

What Was I Thinking?

Controlling my Drinking

One of example of the insanity of alcoholic drinking is the notion that I could control my drinking, that I could drink like a normal person. Many times I came up with a brilliant plan. This plan would work because I believed I was a smart and intelligent man that can solve any problem I am faced with. There was good reason to think in this manner. In all other areas of my life, I was reasonably able to solve the problems I encountered. Therefore, I became arrogant and refused to believe that my drinking was something beyond my means to control. So, of course, I assumed that I could control my drinking. Here are a few insane examples.

The Wine Experiment – One day I decided I was going to switch from hard liquor to wine. Have you ever seen a fight break out and everyone get hauled off to jail as a result of a wine tasting party? I certainly didn't. These people drank in an intelligent and sophisticated manner. So Frank headed off to the liquor store to pick up some wine to sip on slowly and drink out of fancy glasses like a sophisticated well-mannered citizen of the world. Sipping wine and not getting drunk was the solution. Well, I found out those bottles are deceiving. You can only get four glasses of wine out of a bottle. Yes, I got a slight buzz but I was left with that same craving for more and ended up back at the liquor store for another bottle of wine. I just ended up drinking a whole lot more liquid and took many more trips to the bathroom and got just as drunk as any other weekend. The "I will just drink beer" experiment met with similar results. I was living at the urinal and just as drunk.

If you have less available, you will drink less – After the nightly trip to the bar, I would stop at the liquor store and pick up a fifth of whiskey for my wife and me to sip on as we unwound from the day's work. Of course, I was drinking most of the fifth each evening. Since it was there, I would stay up and drink it. A new plan emerged. If I didn't have so much readily available, I wouldn't get so drunk. Therefore, I came up with the brilliant idea of buying just a pint for the evening. I thought, if I don't have a lot, I won't drink a lot. The result will be I won't get as drunk and that was true. Of course when the pint was gone, I wanted more. For two days I resisted the urge to get a bigger nightly bottle. But, in true alcoholic form, of the third day I was back to a fifth of whiskey.

If you can't drink like a normal person, make it appear like you do - Social events are always a challenge for an alcoholic to attend. People just do not know how to drink at social events. These people stand around with their drinks and have intelligent conversations. They have two to four drinks over a four hour period and appear to have fun. These normal drinkers simply baffled me. At the local pub, the boys and I would consistently slam down four drinks an hour and maybe throw in a shot to cap that off. To deal with this lame crowd of pretend drinkers and appear to fit in, I would ensure I was pretty good and lit when I arrived at the social event. I would proceed to drink like them for the four hours pretending to be just like them. After the party, I would make a bee-line to a bar and resume drinking the right way. This is the alcoholic brain on over drive.

Drink myself Sober - During one long drawn out binge, I decided I needed to sober up. At this point stopping cold turkey would result in a dangerous and obvious case of the DT's. So, my alcoholic brain began to form a plan. I was already maintenance drinking during the day at work by sneaking small drinks to keep the tremors a bay until I could get off work and get the true amount of drink I needed. If I could get through an eight hours day with maintenance drinking, maybe I could slowly drink myself sober by drinking just enough to keep from getting sick and then lengthen the time between drinks as time went by. It was a brilliant plan. I would start Friday and be sober by Monday morning. I figured Friday night I would have one drink every two hours for the first evening. On Saturday, I would have one drink every three hours. On Sunday, I would have one drink every four hours. By Monday I would have slowly removed the massive amount of alcohol from my system and would be fine. Well, Friday night I started this disciplined program. Have a drink and then watch the clock. Two hours passed and I took the second drink and again watched the clock. The second two hours passed slower than molasses flowing from a tree in January. Hour six comes and I slam that third drink. Something happened after the six hour mark. All I remember was I passed out drunk yet again. I tried again Saturday morning and ended up drunk again by noon. Sunday I just gave up and got drunk.

I naively tried to beat the addiction with my logic and willpower, losing every time. It wasn't until I admitted that I was powerless over alcohol and surrendered, did I find peace. I had to admit there was no way I could control my drinking by myself. No matter what I tried ended up in yet another failure. I was a slave to alcohol and no brilliant self-conceived plan was going to work.

Four Buckets

Since my sobriety, it has occurred to me that the people in my life can be lumped into four buckets. Each bucket represents how those who know of my quest to stay sober perceive me and how I feel about them.

The first bucket is my fellow recovering drunks who I see at meetings and socialize with on occasion. They are bucket one. They understand me like no other person. They have walked in my shoes and understand the commitment necessary to remain sober. They would drop anything to help a fellow alcoholic in need. When I am with them I feel comfortable in my own skin and am free of all worry. I have serenity in their presence. They don't necessarily trust that I will stay sober; they trust if I work the program I will stay sober.

Bucket two consists of the people in my life who fully support my sobriety. They may not understand the disease and what it takes to stay sober, but they are in my corner and want me to succeed. They desperately want to understand how I could make such a dramatic change from a selfish drunk to a selfless person but can't quite grasp it. They loved me before and try to accept the new me. I so desperately want to not let them down.

Bucket three consists of those people who are happy that I am sober but are waiting for the second shoe to drop. They truly wish for me to remain sober but do not trust that I can. I do not resent those people because I have earned their mistrust. The responsibility for their doubt lies in my past actions. All I can do is remain sober and show them I am a different person today.

In bucket four are those people who want me to fail. They think they need me to fail. They will make comments to me or others that this is a phase and I will be back to my old self soon. They will actively drink in front of me and attempt to bait me to take that first drink. You might think that I resent the bucket 4ers but I do not. They are sick like I was. They feel uncomfortable in my presence because they see me in a place they should be heading to but are not ready to take that first step. They would rather drag me back to their side to justify their actions. All I can do to help them is to remain sober and be ready to talk if they choose to leave their personal hell that I lived in for so long and know all too well.

These are the people in my life and the buckets they fall into. There are shades of gray and a few people sometimes slide between two of the buckets. My actions in the past and my life now define how they perceive me. I am comfortable with all four buckets.

However, there can be a considerable degree of loneliness as I navigate through the seas of this soberly quest. When I am at home or in the workplace, I often feel like the odd man out. Everyone knows what I am trying to do but no one understands. That is why it is so important to stay connected to my fellowship of recovering and recovered alcoholics. It is important not only to see them at the meetings but to make them a part of my daily social life. Integrating the world of recovery and the rest of the world is a difficult but critical balancing act. When I attempt to negotiate the waters alone, the ship begins to keel over and take on water. Staying connected keeps this ship on a steady course.

Random Thoughts

The Greatest

I remember watching Muhammad Ali fight Larry Holmes for the heavyweight championship. Nicknamed The Greatest and arguably one of the greatest fighters of all time, he was taking one last shot at regaining the heavyweight title. It was the most personally painful fight I have ever seen. The once great and brash fighter was being brutally dismantled by Larry Holmes. It is an all too tragic story, an aging athlete trying to win just one more fight. Refusing to admit defeat and face the fact that he just didn't have the ability anymore. This is similar to the Bret Favre analogy I used early in this book. Larry Holmes commented in a later interview that he also was heartbroken to have to end Ali's career in such a manner. He fought to beat Ali but couldn't bring himself to destroy his former sparring partner and hero. Even this pugilistic champion showed a degree of compassion during the fight. At the end, when he had Ali in the corner and knowing he had him beat, he looked to the referee to stop the fight. The referee, torn between giving the legend every chance and his duty to protect the fighter, made the right decision and stopped the brutal onslaught.

Alcohol does not know such compassion. For those who fight on and continue to drink, alcohol will move in for the kill. It will not stop until it kills you in the ring. If you have retired, it will wait patiently for that day you fool heartedly step back into the ring. It won't stop at the bell. There is no referee to stop the fight. Only you can avoid destruction by not starting the fight. If you don't throw in the towel you will die! If I ever decide to get in the ring with alcohol again, I better have my affairs in order because the result will be my death. There will be no glory, no dignity, just death.

More on the Steps

I thought long and hard on how much I should talk about the steps. The steps have been absolutely critical in my gaining and maintaining personal sobriety. However, the steps are a personal journey. The journey will be different for each person. The steps worked for me and each person who decides this technique must work the steps in the manner and pace that works best for them. I will briefly take you through my journey through the steps. The only advice I can give is don't delay and don't half-step when you work them. This is a life and death situation. Work it with someone who understands the steps and has worked them successfully themselves.

Step one - We admitted we were powerless over alcohol - that our lives had become unmanageable.

It amazes me today how long it took me to admit I was powerless over alcohol. The lies I told myself were epic. I would say "I'm not as bad as that guy sitting at the end of the bar," or "Look at her making a fool out of herself." I may drink a lot but, I can handle it. "I'm a functional alcoholic." It was when I couldn't stand to look at myself in the mirror. It was when I had to hide how much I needed to drink. It was when every technique I came up with to limit my intake failed. It was when I could no longer justify sneaking drinks at work to prevent a seizure. It was when I realized that within a few months I would be unemployed, in jail or dead, that I finally admitted that I was totally powerless over alcohol.

Realizing that my life was unmanageable came next. Even though I knew I was powerless, I tried to manage my life with alcohol as the lead in my personal play. It truly was a full time job to ensure I fed my addiction twenty four seven. I tried to balance my drinking career with my job, my marriage, my family, and other responsibilities. It proved to be impossible; the drink had to come first and everything around me took a far second. The only part of my life I was managing was my drinking life and that was killing me. So, I surrendered in a heap of self-pity and begged for help.

Step two - Came to believe that a Power greater than ourselves could restore us to sanity.

I tried to manage it, control it, and use my willpower and everything failed. How could I possibly get sober? Everything I tried was a pathetic failure. Then how could so many alcoholics get and stay sober? Was there a magic pill or special technique? Everyone I spoke with said they stay sober because they accepted a higher power to keep them sober. This was difficult for me to accept. I was an agnostic at best. But, how can thousands of recovering alcoholics be wrong. There was something there and I had to find it. I was so desperate I was willing to try anything. I had to find a higher power to guide me through my recovery. At first my higher power was the program itself. It wasn't much but it was a start. I eventually began to believe in God. I began to become spiritual. I have not joined a church to date, but I can now say "Thy will be done." I ask myself, what God's will is and reject my will. My will got me into this mess and God's will is leading me out of it. Those happy and free recovering alcoholics were right after all. Now, I cannot say for sure what God's will is for me, but I do know drinking is not part of the equation.

Step three - Made a decision to turn our will and our lives over to the care of God as we understood Him.

I struggled with this for a while also. My belief was new and I had doubts. But, all I had to do is decide to try. So, I did. Again, I don't totally understand God and his master plan, but I know what living a good life is. I know what a good person does and acts like and I can only assume, that this must be God's will for me. Doing the right thing for myself and others has reaped rewards that are limitless. They are greater than any monetary or selfish rewards. I realized later that turning my will and my life over to the care of God, as I understood him was the best thing I ever did. I did not lose anything but gained everything. I gave up my way of running my life and adopted God's way. What I lost was fear, worry, resentment, and heartache. What I gained was peace and serenity.

Step four - Made a searching and fearless moral inventory of ourselves.

In this step I looked at my fears, resentments, my sexual conduct, and the harm I did to others in my life. I wrote it all down. I had to drop all resentments I have for people or events because they were a major reason for me to drink. I learned that resentments only hurt me and were basically stupid. Realizing that my time on this earth is short, I decided that I will not waste time replaying resentments in my head anymore. My fears also caused anxiety which in turn gave me an excuse to drink. I looked at all the harm I did to others because of my drinking. Most of the harm I caused was ignoring my responsibilities as a husband, father, employee, and citizen because the drink came first and foremost. This was an incredibly emotional step because I never truly realized how much harm I truly caused as an active alcoholic. The common saying that I only am hurting myself goes away with step 4.

Step five - Admitted to God, to ourselves, and to another human being the exact nature of our wrongs.

I chose my wife to discuss what I learned about myself in step 4. Many use their sponsor. I went over the list again with my sponsor. I found I was more honest with my sponsor. This is also an emotional step. I know of a small few who could get through it in a stoic manner if they truly were honest. To get years of regrets, fears, harms, and resentments off my chest was amazingly liberating and gave me sense that a load was lifted from me. I see this as a dry run to making amends when you get to step 9.

Step six - Were entirely ready to have God remove all these defects of character.

Here I admitted to myself that I had character defects and could not remove them myself. I made a personal commitment to work on my defects daily. I had to realize that it is normal to have defects of character. But, because of the steps I now have the power to choose. I could choose to reject my character defects and try to live in a more selfless manner. I needed the personal courage to admit those defects to myself and do the work to fix them. I needed a higher power to help me with this step.

Step seven - Humbly asked Him to remove our shortcomings.

I took my step four, five, and six and turned it over to God and asked him to remove my defects that caused me to cause harm to others. I asked him to help me live a selfless life. I asked for the power to forgive others and forgive myself. The act of asking for help gave me the feeling of not being alone in this journey. Just asking for them to be removed is step one. I had to recognize and work to fix my defects of character daily.

Step eight - Made a list of all persons we had harmed, and became willing to make amends to them all.

This was easier for me because I did a thorough step four. I find that a good step four sets you up for many other steps. A lackluster step four is a recipe for disaster. I realized that I could not make amends to everyone I hurt in my life but I made the commitment that if the opportunity arose, I would make amends.

Step nine - Made direct amends to such people wherever possible, except when to do so would injure them or others.

I could not track everyone down in my life I needed to make amends to, but I did the best I could. Also, the person you are making amends to do not have to accept your amends. The point is to make the amends. The toughest amends was to my children. They, thankfully for my peace of mind, accepted my apology. The important thing is to do it in an honest manner. I had a problem making amends to my parents because they were deceased. What I chose to do was to write them a letter and put it in an envelope. I taped the envelope to some balloons and released them on Christmas Eve. I watched the balloons rise until they disappeared in my field of vision. What I realized after completing the step was that I was carrying around 300 pound backpack of emotional damage. Once I relieved myself of that enormous weight, I felt free.

Step ten - Continued to take personal inventory and when we were wrong promptly admitted it.

No matter how hard I try to live a good life, I have to realize I am not perfect. I will make mistakes. This step I must do daily and it works. When I do or say something that is wrong, I now realize what I have done and make immediate amends. Think about it, you have already made amends for a lifetime of wrongs, why start building a new list. Before I go to bed, I do a daily inventory. I look at the things I did well such as helping someone with a problem. I also look at the things I did wrong. It could have been a curt word or a selfish act or statement. I make a new personal commitment to do better the next day. Also I learned that I could start my day over in my mind at any time during the day. If things are going wrong and getting out of control, I can just stop. I take a break and reflect, meditate or pray. Then I just start over. For some reason the day gets better.

Step eleven - Sought through prayer and meditation to improve our conscious contact with God *as we understood Him*, praying only for knowledge of His will for us and the power to carry that out.

I start my day saying simply, "Thy Will Be Done." I read the big book and go to meetings. I try to keep in contact with God and live a good life. In the evening, I reflect on my day and try to see where I could have done better. I now often stop during the day to meditate or say a quick prayer. For some reason, I find myself saying a quick prayer while standing at the urinal doing my business. I guess it is as good a time as any because I'm sort of stuck there until I'm done. I've noticed that loneliness has left me. The monster of worries, guilt, anger, and confusion is gone. I feel a presence that is indescribable.

Step twelve - Having had a spiritual awakening as the result of these steps, we tried to carry this message to alcoholics, and to practice these principles in all our affairs.

Writing this is one way to live step twelve. Talking with others that are suffering and especially those who have family members suffering also is my way of doing step twelve daily. Working with others that suffer is the greatest gift we can give. Sponsoring other alcoholics strengthens my program of Sobriety and allows me to give the gift that has been given to me. I am driven daily to help others attain this miracle of Sobriety. It has become a calling. I now understand that my drinking was just one part of my problem. My attitudes and outlook on life and how I fit in to the world was also a problem. My defects of character had to be put into check. I had to stop playing my own personal God and take my proper place in the world. I have to walk the walk in everything I do. I have an enormous responsibility to share this gift with all who desire it. Hopefully, I can continue to grow and be the person I always should have been.

I learned that you don't work the steps once and you're done. I have to work them daily. The day I stop, is the day I relapse. The day I relapse is the day I die spiritually and the day I begin to quickly slide into physical death. I can forgive myself for the past because I didn't know what I didn't know. Now that I have the knowledge, I don't believe I could live with myself if I went back to my drunken life. There is a saying, with knowledge comes responsibility. I chose to be responsible.

The Literature

The wisdom gained from listening to the old timers at meetings is indispensable. An old timer is not someone who is necessarily up in years; it is a person who has been happily and gratefully sober for many years. As they share they always refer to the literature. There are many great books but I feel the following are the most important for someone who is thinking about getting sober or is early in their sobriety. First there is "Alcoholics Anonymous", commonly referred to as the Big Book. The first 164 pages is a blue print to staying sober day by day. Don't just read the book, treat it as a text book that must be studied and followed as directions. Have someone who understands the text teach it too you. Second, there is "The Twelve and Twelve." This is manual for the twelve steps and traditions. It is an excellent companion to the big book. It gives you details of the twelve steps and the traditions. It gives you detailed explanations of how to work them. Another key book is "As Bill See's It" a book of short reflections that can give you a dose of Sobriety in small chunks daily. It is excellent when you have just a few moments and want some reflection.

Oh, and of course, this literary gem that you are holding in your hand is a must read. Ok, that is another character defect coming out. I need to check my ego. Sorry, I'm still a work in progress.

Seriously, these books were not written by a bunch of scholars with three PhD's on their walls with their toughest life challenge to decide whether to play tennis at the club or take the yacht out today. They were written by some drunks just like me. They have walked in my shoes, went through the gates of hell and found their way home. They have proven the saying "It works if you work it." Would you take a sailing lesson from someone who never sailed? I don't know about you, but these books written by my fellow drunks are advice worth reading.

The Pay Raise

Doctors and psychologists may have a lot of fancy book learning on the disease and the human mind however; I and many others like me have found that the best knowledge on alcoholism comes from a fellow recovering alcoholic sharing his or her stories about their own successes and failures. I am not saying that these professionals are not worthwhile. They certainly helped me in the rehabilitation facility. But even most of those were in recovery and walked in my shoes. My advice is to choose you counselor well.

In poorly ventilated back rooms you will find a bunch of recovering drunks sitting around an old table. They are sipping cheap coffee as they try to get comfortable in their metal folding chair. They are freely giving and sharing their experiences and talking about their very real successes and devastating personal failures. This is a far cry from a comfortable psychologist's office. But it is in these meager settings I have found my solution to alcoholism and a new way of living. Many can get help from professionals but most successful recovering alcoholics I've seen find long lasting success from their peers in these rooms.

Many of our lot have fallen into financial debt due to our drinking. The stress of indebtedness can be a trigger to give up on our soberly quest and pick up the bottle again. It was this subject that someone shared this thought. "The biggest pay raise I ever got was the day I quit drinking." The words resonated through me to the core of this drunk's being. As a man of slightly above average means, I was able to maintain my drinking habits and not go bankrupt in the process. I was able to afford my drinks out at the bars and still maintain a stocked liquor cabinet in the house.

My monthly drinking bill was conservatively well over one thousand two hundred dollars a month. During the week it was normal to drop twenty five dollars or more a night at the pub and considerably more on the weekends. My home stock ran me at least another one hundred dollars a week. How does it add up to so much? If someone buys a round of shots, you buy the next. It was just the right thing to do. It is amazing how little you think about how much you spend on booze when you are drinking it. It was almost like a nightly drinking contest. One upping your buddy was the norm. Some of my buddies at the pub would run weekly tabs. I would observe their reaction as they look at their total for the week. They were shocked that they drank that much. Some lost houses, cars, and marriages over their habit.

Imagine my excitement in having an extra fifteen hundred dollars in my pocket each month and not falling that further into debt. In my case, my new found money allowed me to pay debt and actually enabled me to better take care of important things such as family needs and the home. My wife is certainly enjoying the windfall as I witness from the increase of UPS delivery trucks pulling up to the house lately.

I ask myself what was I thinking when I was dropping so much money on alcohol? The truth is I wasn't thinking at all. My disease was doing all the thinking. The monster in my mind was in charge and he was generously serving himself and damn everyone and everything that dared to get in his way. The monster is still in my head. He is still pushing me to go back to my old ways. The difference now is I understand my foe and know how to contain him and I must remember that the minute I get complacent or comfortable, he will attack and I will take that first drink.

Random Thoughts

Turn it over to my Higher Power

It took me a while to figure out what my fellows were talking about when they said "Let Go and Let God" or "Turn your problem over to your Higher Power." They would describe a problem and say "I just turned it over to my higher power to handle." This confused me. Aren't we supposed to solve our own problems? If I lose my job am I supposed to sit on the couch and wait for my higher power to get me a new one? If I am in debt from my drinking career, am I supposed to wait for my higher power to drop money in my lap? Maybe my higher power will deliver me an angel to replace the wife that just dumped me. The answer is of course not! I've since learned by listening, personal action, and experience that it actually means just the opposite. Turning my problem over means to reflect, meditate, or pray on the situation or problem. I gives me the chance to think before I act. I used to just react to problems and generally it just made the problem worse. I must figure out what is the right way to handle whatever problem I am faced with and reflecting before acting generally rears a better result. Sometimes my personal reflection will guide me to directly attack the problem with all my ability. Other times, especially during personality conflicts, the answer is just to let it go because it simply is not all that important in the big picture. I have learned that many personality conflicts that seem imminently important at a given moment can best be handled by leaving it alone and walking away. In almost all cases it turns out it wasn't a big deal to begin with. This also has cleared away a lot of noise and clutter in my daily life. I have learned that these sayings "Let Go, Let God" and "Turn it over to my higher power" breaks down simply as "Do the Right Thing." I also had to realize that I have to deal with life on life's terms. Not everything is supposed to go my way. I don't need to create, fight and win every battle I stumble upon. I am not special. I am just another human being on this earth. This is humility. The world will come at me with successes, failures, problems and tragedy whether I am drunk or not. The difference is I am now better equipped to handle what life throws at me and I am doing far less to create problems for myself.

So turning it over means I am not going to do things my way anymore. My way brought me to the brink of death. I now attempt to do things God's way and things turn out much better. In turning over my will and my life to God, I lose nothing and gain everything. It is the best deal I ever made!

Recover and They Will Come

Being open about my recovery has allowed me to become comfortable with myself, my disease, and my life. I choose to be an open book because I spent so many years hiding behind many different masks. There is a certain amount of freedom and peace of mind in taking off the mask and exposing myself unapologetically to the world. I have found my openness has inadvertently invited many visits and personal calls to inquire about the disease. Some are from people seeking help for themselves; however, many are from people asking advice on how to deal with a family member who they are concerned about. One horrible side effect of the disease is that it affects everyone associated with the alcoholic or addict. His or her actions often cause turmoil within the family. Often times the alcoholic does not realize the pain and anguish his actions have caused. I have found that when an alcoholic is confronted, the most common answer is, "I am not hurting anyone but myself." In fact that statement could not be farther from the truth.

When I am approached by another alcoholic or someone who is concerned about possibly having a drinking problem, the conversation is easy. I simply talk about myself, my struggles, and my experiences. I talk about the feelings of guilt, shame, and loneliness. I discuss the false assumption I made that no one will understand and that there is no way out. I then describe my path to sobriety and what I do each day to stay sober. Finally I offer assistance. Sometimes it works and sometimes it doesn't. But trying to help another person helps me stay strong in my sobriety.

When approached by a family member or friend of someone with a drinking problem the message is not as easy or hopeful. I let them know that alcoholics generally do not want to hear people telling them they have a problem. They certainly do not want to hear how their actions are affecting those around them. I certainly didn't want to hear it and the more people pressed me the harder I drank. I tell these people that they should try to love the alcoholic and hate the disease. I tell them that each alcoholic has to hit his or her own bottom and make a personal decision when enough is enough. I ask them to try not to enable the alcoholic. This may mean putting the alcoholic person out of the home or cutting off relations. I reinforce that the alcoholic may never recover and may end up in prison, homeless, mental institutions, or in an early grave. I express to them that the situation is not their fault and they should try not to feel guilty because they are dealing with someone who is truly ill. Finally, I tell them about support groups for those who are dealing with an alcoholic in their life. My door is always open to help; I can never be too busy to lend a friendly ear.

A Story I wrote for those who have a loved one suffering with an Addiction

THE MIDDLE OF THE LAKE
A Short Story about Enabling

A young boy was born to two good parents. They raised him well, taught him manners and the importance of hard work and education. One day, the mother saw the boy standing by the edge of the lake staring out at the middle. The mother took the opportunity to warn her son not to ever swim out to the middle of the lake because he could drown. All was well.

The boy grew and became a young man. One beautiful spring day the strapping man now twenty was standing by the edge of the lake. He took off his shoes and shirt and dove in and started swimming towards the middle of the lake. He remembered what his mother told him, but he was now a man and could handle anything. When he arrived at the middle of the lake, an incredible euphoria came over him. It was the most wonderful feeling he ever felt. After a while he remembered his mother's warning and swam back to shore.

A week went by and the man was walking by the lake and he remembered how incredible it felt in the middle of the lake. He also thought of his mother's warning. However, he went out there last week and got back safely. He is a man now and can handle the lake. So, he swam out again and the feeling was just as amazing as last time. He stayed longer but was worried his parents would find out and he swam back to shore. Over the next month he would swim out to the middle of the lake once a week.

A few weeks later he would swim out a couple times a week. Not too shortly after that he would go every night. The middle of the lake felt so good. His parents didn't know. He worked the family farm during the day. He told himself he could handle this.

One weekend the family visited close cousins a town over for a two day visit. The young man knew he would miss the lake but also knew it was only a few days. However, a strange thing happened that night. He started to feel sick. The feeling got worse as the night went on. He told his parents he didn't feel well and went home early. When he arrived home he swam back out to the middle of the lake and to his surprise the mysterious sickness went away.

Over time, he spent more and more time in the middle of the lake. In fact, if he was out of the lake for more than a few hours he would get sick. He began to realize he was swimming out to the middle of the lake not to get that wonderful feeling anymore but actually to not feel sick. Nothing mattered to him but the middle of the lake. He started ignoring his responsibilities on the farm and lost interest in his family. His parents noticed the change in his behavior and got worried. They questioned him in an effort to figure this change out. The young man denied that there was any problem.

One evening the mother, so concerned about her son, followed him to the lake. She was shocked and horrified when she saw him swim out to the middle of the lake. She called out to him to swim back. She reminded him how dangerous the middle of the lake was. Now that his secret was out and knowing his mother was right, he embarrassingly swam to shore and promised his mother he would never go into the lake again.

The young man knew his mother was right and made a promise to himself he would stay out of the lake. But, after a very short period of time he began to feel sick again. He tried to fight off the feeling but all he could think of was getting back to the lake. Finally, sick and in pain he stumbled down to the lake and swam out. He immediately felt better and just stayed in the middle of the lake floating and treading water. His parents stood by the edge of the lake calling out to him to swim back. He ignored their calls. He was content and only cared about being in the middle of the lake. His parents stayed by the shore pleading and worrying all night long.

At dawn, the young man grew tired. He began to sink to the bottom of the lake. He called out to his parents to save him. He did not have the energy to swim to shore. His father jumped into a small boat and rowed out, saved his son, and brought him to shore. His mother cleaned him up and fed him and the man regained his strength. Amazingly, and to the shock of his parents, he swam back to the middle of the lake. For weeks on end, the parents would stay by the lake and rescue their son again and again. They feared for his life and hoped he would realize that if this continued he would die soon. Their lives were also falling apart because of their son's actions. His parents argued about what to do.

ENDING NUMBER ONE

The parents loved their son and stayed by the lake day by day. When he would panic and began to drown they saved him. But as soon as he regained his strength he was back in the lake. They noticed over time that the young man was growing weaker and weaker. Finally, one evening the son began to sink again. The father went out to save him but he was gone. The parents were devastated. They always questioned whether they could have handled the situation better.

ENDING NUMBER TWO

The parents loved their son and stayed by the lake day by day. When he would panic and began to drown they saved him. But as soon as he regained his strength he was back in the lake. They noticed over time that the young man was growing weaker and weaker. They never gave up and devoted every moment to saving their son. The farm failed and their life was ruined. They lost touch with family and the community. On their death bed they wondered, who is going to save our son now?

ENDING NUMBER THREE

The parents felt they were enabling their son's ability to keep going back to the lake and decided to not go to the lake anymore. They knew it was a risk, but the only way he would stay out of the lake was to swim out and decide to stay out for good. They were worried sick. Then, their son walked in the house asked his parents for real help and he got better. A few months later his father and the young man drained the lake and all was well again.

ENDING NUMBER FOUR

The parents felt they were enabling their son's ability to keep going back to the lake and decided to not go to the lake anymore. They knew it was a risk, but the only way he would stay out of the lake was to swim out on his own and decide to stay out. They were worried sick. After a while they got word that their son had drowned in the lake. They always questioned whether they could have handled the situation better.

To The Family - There is no right answer and it is not your fault.

Random Thoughts

Top Ten Reasons to Start Drinking Again

1.

2.

3.

4.

5.

6.

7.

8.

9.

10.

Funny,
Can't think of any

The Early Years and Middle Years

The important part of my saga is my fall and fight back to sanity. However, I guess there is some worth in talking about how I got here.

I remember living out on the streets at nine years old drinking beer and stealing purses and running from the cops. My father left when I was two and my mother was in jail. I would rummage through dumpsters to find garbage to eat. Danger lurked at every turn! The world was against me and I was doomed from the start.

Nah!! That sounds exciting but not even close.

I was born to a middle class family in the city of Philadelphia. My parents were loving and supportive. My older sister was the definition of a normal well-adjusted person. Our family lived in a row home. Twenty-six identical houses stuck together with mirror image houses across the street. Behind the houses was a back alley where clotheslines stretched on pulleys thirty feet in the air from your kitchen window to your neighbors across the alley. The streets stretched for miles and miles and for a little kid, it was heaven. The street we lived on was like a big extended family. We called our adult neighbors aunt and uncle. No one locked their doors. There were so many kids on my street that a pick-up game of football had so many players that we had to choose special teams. We played games that only the layout of the street could accommodate. Games like stickball, buck-buck, and wireball were games born from the concrete of the city street. All we needed on those hot summer days was a monkey wrench to open the fire hydrant and we had our own waterpark. Until the police showed up and chased us away. During the summer, whatever house we were playing in front of, that mother would feed everyone lunch. It was an old time Irish/German Catholic neighborhood with all the traditions and trappings that go with it.

Little League baseball, Pop-Warner football, and school was our only reason to leave the block. No one was rich. The fathers worked blue collar jobs and the mothers stayed home and took care of the kids. There was a bar on every corner and a smiling face on every stoop. Drinking was just something our parents did and they were extremely skilled at it. It seemed normal to young kids growing up with alcohol a part of daily life because we knew of nothing else. A typical Saturday night saw the wives sitting in groups on the stoop having a few cocktails and talking. The men would have the card table out playing cards and drinking their beer. The best place to sell stuff for the school fund raiser was the bar on the street corner because that is where everyone hung out. We would play in the street under the watchful eye of the parents. Any parent could whoop any child for misbehaving and we generally deserved a good smack now and then. The best movies to describe the era and the life are "Invincible", "Sleepers", and a "Bronx Tale."

It could be described as a classic mafia style setting but with Irishmen and Germans running the show. Who you were and how you were respected as a kid was determined by how well and often you would fight. Who you knew and how you carried yourself determined what job you would get out of high school. The big one was getting into the sprinkler fitters union.

My little league coach ran that union. He was a Dad, a coach, and one man you did not want to cross. It was not uncommon to see politicians meeting in back rooms of pubs to drum up support for their local campaign. Everything of importance was done with a drink. So, it was understandable that we kids started drinking at a very young age.

My first high school job was at the beer distributor. I got that job because my father was tight with the owner. In those days, you could only buy beer from these beer warehouses and liquor at the state run store. Here is where I got a taste for beer. Beer was only sold by the case and when a case broke, it was ours to drink. We made sure more than a few cases broke each week. I also learned how to run envelopes with cash to the backrooms of businesses and not ask questions. Slipping an envelope into a cop car and a few cases of beer into the trunk of the cruiser was normal business in the neighborhood. Even the local parish rectory and convent received weekly deliveries of beer. The whole place worked on under the table cash, backroom deals, and plenty of booze. The neighborhood worked hard during the day, drank hard at night, and went to church on Sunday. The city had an obsession with the Phillies, Eagles, Flyers, and 76er's. It was a unique world. It was similar to what a kid from Brooklyn, NY might describe if he was from our era. That was life in Philly. Yes, we did throw snowballs at Santa during an Eagles game. I think my Dad took me to that game. Many of my childhood friends still hang out at the same local pubs just as their fathers did many years ago. Some are no longer with us.

Being a decent high school football player took me on a different path and away from the trappings of the neighborhood. I managed to get accepted to a division three football school and left the old neighborhood. The college years were, from what I can remember, a blast. The priorities were women, drinking, sports, parties, fraternity, and as a necessary nuisance we dealt with school. Drinking every day was simply a way of life. Our whole social experience started with, was engulfed by, and ended with an endless supply of cheap liquor and beer. My college experience mirrored the movie "Animal House" on a daily basis. I spent three years on academic probation and a year and a half on disciplinary probation. That time of my life could be another story in itself. College did give me the ROTC program and a commission in the Army. I got married upon graduation and went on active duty to serve my country as a Lieutenant in the Army.

I assumed that being in the Army meant the party was over. It was time to be responsible and start a family. The party wasn't over; it just changed. Army life prevented me from drinking every day, especially during field training exercises and deployments. So, I became a master of binge drinking at every opportunity. The practice of staying out until 4AM drinking, coming to work at 5AM, then running three miles, puking, showering, and going to work was normal. Just like my parents in the old neighborhood, "work hard and play hard" was our motto.

Not every Soldier in the Army drank like my buddies and I did. But birds of a feather flock together. No matter where I was stationed, I would smell out my fellow drinkers. It wouldn't take long to assemble a posse of drinkers or to join the drinkers in the unit I was assigned to. Moving every three years in the Army gave me a fresh start. New pubs, new drinking buddies, and new local brews were all fresh adventures to be experienced. I managed to have a respectable career and fathered two lovely daughters. At this point, I did not see a problem. In fact, it was normal. Or at least I thought it was.

My career ended at the fourteen year mark because of a divorce and I was growing weary of the daily grind of Army life. I always wondered if my professional drinking added to my weariness or at least was starting to cloud my sense of reality. However, I immediately got a Department of the Army civilian job which I still have as I write this section. This allowed me to drink much more freely and at will. I also got re-married to my best drinking buddy ever. She was a Soldier also, and we continued to live the Army life. Despite marriage and career changes, the only thing that didn't change was my drinking.

It is hard to pin-point the exact day the drinking caught up with me. It was more like a slow decline deeper and deeper into alcoholism. I didn't see it coming. It snuck up on me like a thief in the night. What I can say is, I dealt with a series of life events over a three year period and I tried drinking them away. When life got tough, I drank.

When my father got sick and finally passed, I medicated myself with the bottle. When my wife deployed to the middle-east for a year in 2006 and left me with six teenagers (four lived with me daily and my two were out in the summer and every holiday), I drank. Controlling six teenagers as a temporary single parent was like herding kittens. If one got out of the box, I would go find it and upon my return, two more were missing. So of course, I drank more. When my wife returned she had a massive stroke. It almost killed her. I spent every moment by her side. I didn't leave the hospital or shower for weeks. I was her rock and Jack Daniels was mine. I drank constantly. I hid my bottle in her Army boot in the hospital closet. This is an example of the alcoholic brain at work. When she was released from the hospital, I took her directly to the pub. I told her that her friends wanted to see her. Of course they did, but I also wanted to get our daily pub routine back on track. She was off work a year for recovery. I ensured when I got home from work that I got her out of the house. Most of the time it was off to the pub to hang out, talk and of course drink. The Pub was my real home. It was my sanctuary from life. When it was time to step up as a father, a husband, and a man, I hid in the bottle. I did meet most of my basic responsibilities but they were second to the bottle. At the time, I thought it was normal, life threw problems at me and I deserved to drink. No one had a life like I had. I had a highly demanding job; six kids and a sick wife to take care of. I deserved to drink and who wouldn't if they had to deal with what I had to. There is a saying around the sober club that some of the old timers throw out to the whiners. "Pour me, pour me, pour me another drink." That was me! As I look back now, I realize how far down the alcohol took me. It warped my sense of reality.

Acceptance

Acceptance has been a major key to my recovery. Without it, I would be still out there drinking myself to death, or either be dead broke or in jail. The first thing I had to accept is that I am truly powerless over alcohol. Alcohol was the master and I was the slave. Accepting that fact allowed me to be honest with myself and understand that I had a big problem. Then I had to accept that the problem was an incurable disease of my body and mind. I had to have a full knowledge of my condition. Then I had to accept that I could not handle this disease on my own. I had to accept help from others. My others were a sponsor, fellow drunks in successful recovery, and a higher power of my understanding.

Once that was working, I had to accept that if I didn't treat my disease every day, I would surely drink again. I had to accept that when I wake up every morning I am granted only a daily reprieve. Today, I am sober. If I don't drink today, I won't get drunk. Yesterday is gone, tomorrow is not a guarantee, and all I have is today. I must accept that if I don't give it away or give back, and help others recover, there will be a hole in my recovery. Finally, and most importantly, I have to absolutely accept each day that I will always be an alcoholic until the day I die. The day I think I have this disease beat, is the day the disease will come out of hiding and I will drink again.

So, I have stopped lying and bargaining with myself. I have stopped hoping that somehow everything will be magically fixed and I just accepted what and who I am and make a daily commitment do what I need to do each day to stay sober. Finally, I try to keep it simple. If I don't take that first drink, I won't get drunk.

Random Thoughts

Ice Cream

One technique I learned early in recovery to reduce my craving for alcohol was to eat sweets. I don't know why it works or if it works for everyone, but it sure worked for this drunk. A piece of candy seemed to ease my craving to drink. I eventually settled on ice cream. I always loved ice cream as a child but didn't touch it for years, simply because ice cream took up too much room in my stomach and didn't go well with whiskey or beer. A bowl of ice cream every evening satisfied my craving for the drink. During the day a candy bar would also help. It became as routine as my nightly Jack Daniels on the rocks in front of the TV. Every evening about 8pm I would meticulously prepare a heaping bowl of ice cream with a splash of milk on top. I would mix it into a gooey milk shake like concoction and slowly eat the sloppy potion with a spoon. I would sip it off the spoon like a Jack Daniels on the rocks. For some reason, any craving I had would be satisfied. Oh, I also put on a few extra pounds. For a good while I believed I was becoming addicted to ice cream. Actually, Reese's Peanut Butter Ice Cream was my new drug of choice. I loved it just like my Jack Daniels. After a while, my need for ice cream faded from a daily replacement for alcohol to an occasional treat.

Thank God for Ice Cream

Gratitude

Feelings of self-pity and depression can haunt a recovering alcoholic, especially early in recovery. Once the head is clear, an alcoholic begins to realize the harms he has done to others during his drinking career. Total forgiveness of those who harmed me and forgiveness of myself was critical step in my personal recovery. However, once the forgiving phase is complete we are faced with life. Just because you are sober does not mean that life will be a series of peaceful walks on the beach without a care or worry in the world. On the contrary life will continue to be hard, cruel, and often unfair. Disappointment, hard knocks, and tragedy will still befall us whether we are drunk or sober. When I was drinking, issues and problems became another excuse to drink and often drink harder. I used to believe unfair wrongs had been done to me and a drink was the least I deserved for dealing with my horrible life. In retrospect, drinking only delayed dealing with a pressing problem and often made the problem worse. I now accept that problems and issues will crop up every day. Welcome to life, it is here and it is real. I now deal with life with a sober head and refuse to wallow in self-pity.

Gratitude is now a part of my life and my thoughts on a daily basis. The feelings of gratitude eluded me most my adult life. Now I have a balance sheet. When things go wrong, as they most certainly always will, I turn to my gratitude list and realize that despite life's challenges, I have a lot to be grateful for. My gratitude list starts with the simple things. I woke up today. I woke up today sober. I have a roof over my head. I have people who care about me. The list goes on and on. So when my boss is an asshole today, I deal with it and put it in perspective. It could be a lot worse. I am most grateful that no one or nothing I encounter today is so horrible or overwhelming that I have to drink over it. I am grateful and that makes me happy. I have some peace and serenity.

My wife once asked, what does sober stand for? I told her it doesn't stand for anything. She said maybe it means this: SOBER – Son of a bitch everything's real. I like that and I can deal with it too.

What was I Thinking?

College

College is a time when you take that first step to leave the protective nest of family and the neighborhood and begin an academic and socially enriching journey that will set you up to make a positive difference in the world. Or, in my fraternity brothers' and my case, it was a time to remake the movie "Animal House" on a daily basis. When I look back, I can honestly ask, "What were we thinking and how the hell could we still be alive?" It is not an exaggeration to believe they let us graduate just to get rid of our crazy delinquent asses. Here are just a few examples.

Fraternity - There were no fraternities on campus so we figured we would start one up and we did. It took about a year for all the kids who were there to party and chase women to be drawn together in this wild alliance. Once together we started a fraternity. The purpose of a fraternity is academic excellence, community service, brotherly love, and social merit. For this bunch of future alcoholics it was means to legitimize our thenty four seven party.

Let's make a golf course – One drunken night about three AM we were driving golf balls from the back of our building into the parking lot. We had two problems. First we were drunk and second there were a bunch of trees in the way and we could not achieve our academic goal of destroying cars with golf balls. One of our brothers solved the problem by bringing his chainsaw back the next night so we could cut down seven or eight trees in order to have a clear fairway to the parking lot. What were we thinking?

Pledge Bowling - One night one of us came up with the brilliant idea to play pledge bowling. We got a keg of beer, cups, pledges, and we all got good and drunk. We put the kegs at the bottom of a hill and lined the pledges up as bowling pins. We had them stand on one foot with a full cup of beer in their right hand. Then we had another pledge hurl his body down the hill in an attempt to slam into the human pledge pins and spill the beer. If your beer spilled you had to chug your beer. The human bowling ball had to drink all the beers that didn't spill. The result was some puking, two twisted ankles, a few scraped knees, and one trip to the hospital. What were we thinking?

You Must Have Rules – Six of us lived in a suite in one of the buildings. This is college so we had some rules we concocted to have the right to live in our suite. By God, this is an academic institution there had to be rules, laws, and order! The most important rule was no books or studying allowed. One night one of our brothers locked himself in his room and was studying for an accounting exam. When we noticed he wasn't in the common area drinking, we investigated. To our horror we found out he was studying. We pleaded with him to stop and get drunk with us but he refused. We had no choice but to grab baseball bats and knock the door handle off the door and drag him out of his room. We had to save him from himself. Of course he came to his senses and got drunk. In retribution he smashed the handles off all our doors to save us too. Problem solved! What were we thinking?

Bring us a Dead Body - One quiet night we were sitting around drinking and found out one of our pledges worked for a funeral home. Of course we assembled all the pledges and announced that we wanted a dead body delivered to us by dawn. After a solid night of drinking we were awakened by a hearse backed up to our sliding glass door with a recently deceased old woman in the back. What were we thinking?

These Girls are Snobs - The girls from the sorority in the next building hated us. They had a warped sense of college. They were there to get an education. They didn't go to our parties and would not have sex with us on demand. There was something wrong with them. So, we had to take action. First, we bought 200 mice and released them in their building. They still wouldn't sleep with us. Then we had a party and accidentally broke 80% of the windows in their building. They still didn't come around. Finally on Valentine's Day, we had our pledges hand deliver boxes of contraceptive foam wrapped in abortion ad paper. The dean decided to put us on disciplinary probation for a year after that gesture. Funny, they never slept with us. What were we thinking?

The Wall – The common area of our suites was probably twice the size of an average living room. It was a cinder block room with a Budweiser neon sign on the wall. We decided it was time to redecorate. After hours of academic debate over a dozen beers, we made the decision. For the entire semester, we would only drink Bud cans and glue the empty cans to the wall from floor to ceiling. Our accounting major determined it would take about a thousand cases of beer to complete the task. Some doubted we could do it, but we were academic masterminds and we accomplished the task in a few months. Initially, we washed the cans out before gluing them to the wall. But, after a day we were gluing half drank cans, and cans with cigarette butts to the wall. It was beautiful. Some visitors thought it smelled. We never noticed. When we took them down at the end of the year we put them in one of our fraternity brother's unlocked VW bug in the parking lot. I think he had to sell the car. What were we thinking?

Suite Wrecking Party - At the end of our sophomore year, the college brass thought it would be best for the student body to break-up six of the most notorious of our emerging fraternity. Upper classmen lived in buildings that contained what was referred to as suites. Each suite consisted of three two man rooms, a bathroom and a living room. Since the administration was not allowing the six to live together the next year, we had to take action. Since they couldn't live there, we decided that no one could ever live there again. Thus the concept of the suite wrecking party was dreamed up one drunken night.

For a week leading up to the party, cleanliness and hygiene in the suite was forgotten. Trash and beer cans started to pile up in preparation of the act of personal freedom and anarchy. The night of the party came and the booze was flying. It was literally flying as every beer bottle drank was smash against the wall, the floor, or a poor freshman's head. That was the night I became famous for chugging three quarters of a quart of vodka in five minutes and did not puke or pass out. That probably should have been a hint that I was an alcoholic. The party was epic. All the doors were torn from their frames. Two sinks were torn from the wall. Graffiti was artistically placed on the walls. The carpet was stained, burned, and as a last act of defiance defecated on. The place looked like a war zone. We all left for summer convinced we had stuck it to the man. Until the damage bill came in the mail and there was a lot of explaining to do to the parents that got the bill. What were we thinking?

We all got back together in building nine the next year through some suspect campus contacts and as a bonus we had a party patio built outside the building. After two years in the building our group of now seniors repeated the suite wrecking party prior to graduation which was highlighted by our couch being set on fire and thrown out of the third story window. Also a rumor started by us that we were going to blow up the building got us a trip to the Dean of Students office for the "you will go to jail if you blow up the building" chat. As good college students, we learned an important lesson in college. That lesson was simply, cover your ass. So after the second suite wrecking party, we were seasoned academics ready to take on the world. We took the fire hose from the hallway and flooded the suite. It was an epic site seeing beer cans and assorted trash floating around as we finished our beers and went to another party on campus. Upon our return from our evening of academic excellence we called campus security and reported that our suite had been vandalized. There was no bill that summer. What were we thinking?

I could give a few dozen other examples but I think you get the point.

Forgiveness

A dry drunk is a drunk who just doesn't drink. I, as a dry drunk, was a miserable confused person who was impossible to live with. As a result of this misery, I eventually fell back into my old drinking habits. To become truly sober, I not only have to completely abstain from drinking, I must change my perspective on life and how I am supposed to fit into this complex world. As I discussed in addressing character defects, I must recognized my defects and work to fix them. I must be selfish about my sobriety and selfless in all my affairs.

Another thing I had to do was to forgive myself and drop my resentments for others who have hurt me. First, I had to forgive myself for the wrongs I did others while I was an active alcoholic. The steps helped me to recall them, admit them, and finally make amends for them. This process helped my personal healing and self-forgiveness. Understanding that I am flawed and not unique, I can now recognize when I act or speak in a manner that is hurtful to another human being. I can catch myself and correct my behavior. If necessary, I can make immediate amends. This allows me to not have that two thousand pound sack of regrets, resentments, and fears I used to carry around for years. That sack most certainly fueled my drinking. I try to empty a now small sack every day so I can start the next day with a clean slate.

Dropping resentments for others who hurt me was also necessary to maintain my sobriety. Anger and resentment fuels self-pity and at least for this drunk it was just another lame excuse to justify my drinking. I began to realize that many of the people who did me harm were sick themselves. They, like all human beings, have character defects. Holding resentment against them was just punishing me daily by reliving something that was done to me possibly years before. In fact most people who had done something to harm me probably don't even remember the statement or event. It sounds silly now to hold a hatred or resentment, but I did and I know of many who carry resentments around resulting in their own misery today.

So I dropped all my resentments and said "live and let live" and my life is better. I cleared my brain of useless thoughts that just don't matter anymore.

Well, except this one big resentment. There was a resentment I could not let go of. To let this one go would be the greatest personal challenge of my recovery. I struggled and pondered long and hard whether to talk about it in this book. Is it too personal? Is it appropriate? But it is a part of my recovery, so here it is.

It is hard to pin down my exact age when it happened. I believe I was about seven or eight years old. Two teenage boys from the neighborhood, who I knew well and in fact, were known as just two of the many kids on the block, committed an act that has haunted me for years. One day they approached me and asked if I wanted to join their street hockey team. They thought I would make a great goalie. Imagine my excitement when these big guys were interested in me. Of course, I agreed. They told me I had to try out for the team and I needed to come with them. So, down into one of the boy's basement on my block we went. In the basement was a hockey net and gear. I spent some time blocking shots and receiving praise from these godlike teens. When we finished they announced that I made the team and I was beyond excited. They stated that I had to go through the secret ceremony that everyone on the team had to go through. I of course agreed.

What happened next was frightening, painful, brutal, confusing, and left a mark on me for life. I was taken to the laundry area where I was de-panted, bent over the washer, held down and raped. I remember my feet reaching for the floor only finding air. When it was over I was told it was all a joke, there was no team. I was warned that if I said anything, they would do it again and kill me this time.

I had no real understanding of what had just happened to me. I was only seven or eight years old. All I knew was fear and confusion. I thought if I told my parents, I would somehow be in trouble. So, I said nothing. I tucked it deep down and did not think of it for years. The defense mechanism in the mind is an amazing thing. It protected me from the memory for a while. Only for a while!

As an adult, something triggered my memory of that day. I believe it was a TV report on a pedophile. The event came rushing back to me in feelings of anger, hatred, and fear. Possibly like a Soldier suffering a post-traumatic stress disorder experiences an episode. Oh yes, this was a resentment. This is how I handled this resentment. I would relive the event in my mind. I wouldn't every day but very often. I would fantasize what I would do to them if I ever saw them again. I didn't want to hurt them. I wanted capture them and torture them for days. I wanted them to slowly die before my eyes in the most brutal manner I could imagine. Did I mention I was holding resentment? This was not just a fantasy, it was a plan. I spent countless hours searching the internet trying to find one of them. If I found him, I would act. I didn't care that I would spend the rest of my life in jail for getting my revenge. In my mind the sweet revenge was worth any price.

Being computer savvy, I was frustrated that I couldn't track this person down. I imagine I could have if I was more public in my search but I wasn't going to let anyone know my secret. When I was in the rehabilitation facility, going through the steps and listing and dropping my resentments, I had trouble dropping this one. I discussed the resentment with a counselor who told me to pray for the boys who raped me every night for a week and I would drop the resentment. After a week of prayer, I told him I didn't want to kill them anymore, but I still wanted to smash their kneecaps with a baseball bat. It was a little improvement but I certainly didn't drop the resentment.

What is interesting about recovery is that a breakthrough comes to people sometimes quickly and sometimes slowly. Often, others see the change in you before you see it in yourself. This was true in my case. One day, when I was about six months sober, I was innocently looking at my Facebook account. I noticed that one of my childhood friends had a mutual friend who happened to be the rapist's little brother. My years of searching had been in vain because I misspelled the last name by one letter. Now, I finally had the lead I sought for so many years to find him and exact my revenge. I calmly shut down the page on my computer and went about my business. I had dropped the resentment that drove my passion and thoughts. I am sober with a new outlook on life. It was on that day that I was absolutely sure that what I was doing to stay sober not only keeps me from being a drunk but also makes me a better person. I am not saying that I still don't think about that horrible day and that frightened brutalized little boy, I just accept it and decided it will not cripple me.

It's Alive, It's Alive

I am firmly convinced that this disease is not only alive within me, but that it also is an intelligent entity that is always ready to strike. It is often described as cunning foe and will attempt to confuse you at every turn. My disease only reveals just enough of itself to me to have its desired effect. In my early day of drinking, the disease only had to tell me that drinking was fun. It revealed to me that I can be more confident, popular, and attractive. When I started to get into some trouble due to my drinking, the disease told me it was someone else's fault and I deserved to have this fun. When some of my goals and dreams were cut down by the drink, my disease convinced me that my dreams were not worth the effort. When adult responsibilities were getting in the way of my drinking, the disease told me that people are asking too much of me and I should be left alone. When I started to realize that the drink was causing harm to my life, my health, and my future and I tried to control my drinking, my disease waited for my triggers to pop-up and it told me to drink. The triggers were fear, anger, frustration, doubt, and all those things in life that makes one feel uneasy. The disease spent many years convincing me that the only way to deal with life was with a good stiff drink and I was more than willing to oblige my diseases hints, suggestions, and demands.

When I finally hit my last and hopefully final bottom and became sober, I did something that kicked my disease in the gut. I made it so the disease couldn't reach me. I found out what to do to. I surrounded myself with other recovering alcoholics. I worked the steps with my sponsor. I found a higher power of my understanding and stayed in touch with my fellowship and my higher power on a daily basis. I made prayer and meditation a part of my life. I changed the way I approach life and became more selfless and less selfish. I began to help others who are still suffering by sharing my experience, strength, and hope in meetings and by sponsoring other alcoholics. I became part of the world, my community, and my fellowship and decided I was not going to be the self-perceived center of the universe. I recovered, but I am by no means cured.

The disease still exists inside me. It is just waiting patiently for me to stop doing those daily things that shield me from the claws of the disease. It is waiting for me to get cocky and overconfident. It is waiting me to think that I am keeping myself sober and I don't need to do all those critical things that got me to this point. It is waiting for me to walk away from what works and stroll down that dark alley in my brain. It is waiting for me isolate myself. Then the disease will appear and strike. It will be me against him and I will lose. I need my posse of my higher power, my fellows, and the steps, working as one unit to win on a daily basis.

Random Thoughts

Would you like to stay Sober? Hang Out With a Bunch of Drunks

All my adult life I hung out with my fellow drunks. No matter where I was, I would sniff them out and they me. In most cases we would fast become drinking buddies. We would become each other's counselors, friends, and companions. Occasionally, a few fists would fly and in most cases, we would drink and laugh about the fight. Drunks feel most comfortable drinking and socializing with other drunks. It makes sense. A drunk is not going to look down on another drunk. They hang out in pubs together. They go to ballgames together. They share the same passion. That passion they share is alcohol. They are not going to say "hey buddy maybe you should slow down" or "think about quitting drinking." They are the best of friends. However, take alcohol away from just one and the friendship will disappear quicker than a light being shut off. The alcohol is the bond that holds the relationship together. Without it, these friends become strangers that would not recognize each other and probably wonder why they were ever friends in the first place.

I and many other successful recovering alcoholics have realized that we too must be with fellow drunks to stay sober. In this case, the fellow drunks are also in recovery. Just like two drunks hanging out in a bar drinking, drunks in recovery hang out and talk about not drinking. They share their stories of their crazy and tragic past. They also talk about the same things active alcoholics talk about in the bars. My fellows and I talk sports, politics, current events, and weather. We are just not drinking or drunk anymore. We also tend to make a little more sense and tend not to constantly repeat ourselves and pass out. We in recovery also do not judge each other. We tell our story and no one judges. There is nothing we can tell each other that would shock any of us. We help and watch out for each other. We constantly and freely remind each other of the mistakes we made in the hope that our experience will prevent our fellow from repeating those same mistakes. We understand that we are not alone. We now know we are not pitiful freaks or bums. We realize that we are blessed to have such incredible understanding and support. I am most comfortable in my skin and most confident in my sobriety when I hang out with fellow drunks who don't drink.

Drawing from a Lesson of the Past to Stay Sober

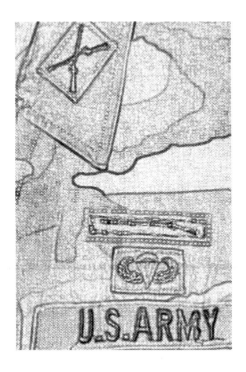

It is difficult to describe the feelings of happiness, serenity, and freedom sobriety has given me. There was a time when I could never imagine a life without drinking. Now I can't imagine ever living the life of a drunk again. These feelings are a daily reminder of why I never want to go back to the life of an active drinker.

What I had to do and how I realized what needed to be done was learned through a series of trials and errors. When I figured out how to get and stay sober, I realized I learned the lesson years before from a totally unrelated challenge but I could not see the forest for the trees.

When I was in the Army there was a prestigious badge that Infantrymen competed for. It was the Expert Infantryman Badge (EIB). To be awarded the EIB, the soldier had to successfully complete a number of prerequisites and pass a battery, in fact dozens of physical and mental graded tests on basic infantry skills. The test culminated with a forced road march that consisted of a twelve mile road march, carrying an M16 rifle and a thirty five pound load plus extra gear for a total of up to seventy pounds. The march had to be completed within three hours. The EIB test was administered on average once per year with pass rates only around ten percent. Every Infantryman wanted the honor to wear this badge on their uniform and I was no exception.

The first time I attempted the test I wanted the badge. However, I did not put the necessary study and work into preparing for the three day event. The result was failing the event miserably. If memory serves, I was drummed out very early in the first day. I blamed the graders, the test, and everyone else but me for the failure.

The second time I tried for the Expert Infantryman Badge, I went from wanting it to really wanting it I and put more effort into preparing for the test. This resulted in a better effort but a second failure. Again, my failure was rationalized by excuses. The third time I really wanted to get the coveted badge and was finally willing and ready to do anything it took to get it. This time I moved out of my house a week prior to the test. I left my wife and children behind to ensure I was focused on this one goal. I moved into the arms room at my unit and surrounded myself with all the weapons and equipment I was to be tested on. I slept in the arms room on a cot and made sure I had no distractions. There was no TV, radio, or cell phone. It was just me and my goal. I had a singleness of purpose. This time the result was I completed the three day event and earned the Expert Infantryman Badge.

My battle to overcome alcoholism in some way is a parallel and a very similar story line. Early attempts to stop drinking were failures. I wanted to stop but I wasn't willing to make the hard choices and do what was truly necessary to stop. Attempts to control how much I drank at a given sitting met with failure after failure. Switching from hard liquor to beer or wine didn't work. I also tried to space out the time between drinks in an attempt to reduce my dependency. All of these techniques garnished the same result. I got drunk. Just like the Expert Infantryman's Badge, it was the result I got from wanting something but not being willing to do what was necessary to achieve the goal.

One day I really wanted to stop drinking and was willing to do some serious things to get sober. I decided to abstain from liquor completely and attend AA meetings. This was a result of my second trip to the hospital. Generally my ass was on fire when I gave sobriety a try. Although I went to AA, I wasn't willing to get a sponsor. I chose not to read and study the literature. I knew of the twelve steps but I only applied the ones that I thought applied to me and those happened to be the ones that required little or no effort. Just like my second attempt at the Expert Infantryman Badge, I did okay for a while but ultimately failed and got and stayed drunk yet again.

Finally, I really wanted to get sober and I was finally ready to do absolutely anything to achieve my goal. Yes, my ass was on fire again. This time I was truly sick and tired of being sick and tired. Just like my successful attempt to earn that coveted badge, I again left my wife and family, not to train for a test, but to check into a rehabilitation center. I came clean to my boss at work. Perceptions of my family, my friends, and my co-workers didn't matter. I had to get sober or die. This had to be the only thing in my life at that moment. After REHAB I went directly back to AA. This time I got a sponsor. I read everything on the subject of my disease I could get my hands on. I worked the twelve steps and when I finished, I worked them again. This time I got sober. Just like the Expert Infantryman Badge, it wasn't until I really wanted sobriety and was fully ready to do anything to get sober, success came my way. It was the only way I was going to get well.

There is one difference in my two stories. Once I got the Infantryman badge, I had it for life. I have a plaque that hangs on the wall. My military record will show my achievement long after I have left the earth. No one can ever take away what I achieved. This is not true for my sobriety. To keep it, I have to work my program of recovery every day. If I make maintaining my sobriety my first priority, then happiness, joyfulness, peace of mind, and serenity will follow. I hate to always end on a note of warning but the minute I get complacent, cocky, and drift from my program I will get drunk and destroy all that I have worked so hard for.

The Dream

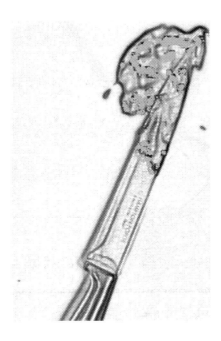

When I was a child I had a recurring dream about alcohol. It was long before I took my first drink. My parents loved their beer. They drank beer every night and more on the weekends. In our family, drinking was what appeared to be the reward for a hard day's work. Beer was just a part of our family life. Getting my Mom or Dad a beer from the fridge was as normal as taking out the trash. Going with my Dad every Friday to the beer distributer and paying his beer delivery bill and then picking up a few cases for the weekend was just plain normal. There were never any arguments or violence in my house. I never saw them fall down or pass out. Therefore, drinking was a normal innocuous activity for grownups.

I now sometimes reflect back on the dream I had as a child. In a house with no outward stress or violence, this dream became part of my psyche and still haunts me today.

The Dream

It is my mother's fiftieth birthday party. I am seven or eight years old. All the neighborhood adults are at the house for a huge birthday party. Everyone is drinking, laughing and singing along with Nat King Cole and Frank Sinatra records on the huge console record player. They are having their usual good time. Someone, I believe my older sister, makes a pyramid of fifty bottles of Ballantine beer shaped as a birthday cake for my Mom. All this actually happened once on her actual birthday. In the dream, my mother asks me to get her a beer. I go to the refrigerator, take out a sixteen ounce bottle of beer, and walk it through the crowd of party goers to find my mom. I find her by the actual birthday cake that she is about to cut. I reach the beer up to her and when she moves to grab it, the beer slips out of my hand and shatters on the floor. The room goes silent as all eyes are on me. I look up in fear at my mother and see that she has grabbed the knife and is beginning to stab me for dropping the beer. That is when I would wake up in terror. I never understood the dream. My mother was sweet, loving, and kind. Yes, she loved her beer but not so much to kill over it. I don't know how or if the dream has any meaning on my alcoholism but it is part of my story. All I know is that drinking was a normal and necessary part of life instilled in me at a very early age.

Living in a Drinking World

It is virtually impossible for the recovering alcoholic to live out the rest of his or her life completely divorced from the sights, smells, and contact with alcohol. Let's face it alcohol is a part of our culture.

From the first date to the wedding toast, from sneaking that first drink as a teen to hanging at the pub with the boys, from celebrating the birth of a child to raising your glass to say goodbye to a recently departed friend, alcohol is a way to bring people together for almost any reason. Getting a beer at the ballpark is more American than apple pie. Open a magazine, turn on the TV, take a ride down the road, turn on your computer and you will be quickly inundated with images and advertisements for alcohol. The full page ad will not be an image of a bum passed out in a back alley with a case of beer by his side. It will be beautiful, successful people, gathering in scenes of joy, excitement, camaraderie, and love. They will represent what everyone wants out of life. The people in the advertisement will seem like they are living in heaven itself. You would think alcohol is as critical to life as breathing. So, what the hell should the alcoholic who desperately needs and wants to remain sober do? Unfortunately, there is no magical island we go to live our life out in peace and sober serenity. If there is a sober island out there, some active alcoholics would figure out a way to drink there too and screw it up for everyone. That is what we do. The sights, sounds, and smells of alcohol are here and it will be in our face for the rest of our days. We just have to understand that fact and learn to deal with it. But how do we, the alcoholics, mentally obsessed with drinking, deal with it and not end up drunk?

Everyone deals with this challenge differently so I will not give advice. Each person on this soberly quest must find his or her own technique to live in an alcohol crazy world. This is how I dealt and deal with it on a daily basis. Remember, this is a one day at a time quest. If I fall asleep sober today, I am a winner. First I was sick enough that I needed to place myself in a rehabilitation facility. I needed to safely get over the physical addiction and then be totally cut off from the temptation and access to alcohol. But, we can't stay locked up forever. We must emerge from the safety of the REHAB facility and re-join our world. I decided I needed to immediately change some things. Daily trips to the pub had to stop. In the past, I tried to stay sober and go to the pub to hang out and it ended in total drunken disaster. The pub life was the first to go. I stopped going to bars and restaurants for the sole purpose of meeting for drinks. If it was a dinner event, then I would go. I always got myself there so that I could leave if the urge was too strong. I wouldn't let myself get caught in any situation without an exit plan. The exit plan saved my ass a number of times early in my sobriety. I was always very upfront with people I was with that I am an alcoholic and will not drink. I found it was harder to hide my condition and make excuses. This is also a personal choice. I also have the additional challenge of living with an active drinker. I thought long and hard about asking my wife not to have or drink alcohol in the house. In fact we discussed it a few times. The bottom line was my realization that I have the problem and why should she change her life because of me. So, I have chosen to live a sober life with alcohol always a few steps away. Many relationships do and need to end for one partner to remain sober and save his or her own life. So far, my situation is manageable. It is not easy but I am dealing with it. Here is how I put living with a drinker into perspective in my mind. Let's say I was allergic to eating peanut butter, who am I to make the holy decree that no one living in my home eat peanut butter? No, that would be absurd. The peanut butter is my poison, certainly not a poison for the entire world.

I had to accept some things. I had to accept the fact that alcohol is not some evil force set upon this earth to destroy the world. Prohibition came and went and changed nothing. Most people can take it or leave it and can drink responsibly if they choose to do so. Alcohol is bad for me. I have this incurable disease. I have to have a full understanding of my disease and what happens to me when I drink. I have to understand that if I drink, I will die. I must ask myself this question before I go to any place that has or serves alcohol. Why am I going? If there is no good reason other than there are people drinking, then I should not go. I had to accept that the disease is countless times stronger than my willpower. If I am not in a good place mentally, spiritually, and emotionally, I should avoid all temptation. I must treat my disease every day by prayer, meditation, attending meetings, and talking to my fellow drunks in recovery. The minute I feel I've got this thing licked, I need to get to a meeting. I can't get complacent or cocky or I will drink again. As long as I do all these things, I can go anywhere and participate in any event and stay sober. I draw upon the inspiration of those new friends that have been sober 10, 20 or even 30 years.

They have been to hell and have found a solution. They are humble and still after decades, come to meetings to listen and share their experience. They will tell us after decades of sobriety that the minute they forget they are an alcoholic and stop working on their recovery, they will get drunk again. They are my heroes, they are my role models. Many of them are your co-workers and neighbors. Unless they confided in you, you would never know they ever had an issue.

One interesting thing happened in my soberly development. When I do decide to go to that concert, ballgame, or work function, I see things much differently than I saw things when I was actively drinking. When I was drinking, everything was normal and fun. If there was an issue, it was someone else's fault. This new experience generally starts out with a lot of happy people gathering together in fellowship. Drinking begins and all is fine, fun and everything appears innocent. After a while, certain people begin to get drunk and especially in large events, things start to break down. Intelligent conversations become stupid and repetitive. Did you ever spend a night with a drunk and he repeats the same statements over and over again and does not even realize it? I used to be that drunk. Back to the event; the noise level rises and things begin to become chaotic. These individuals have taken social drinking to another level. People all of a sudden become less joyful and more agitated. Sometimes arguments or even fights break out. This is when I now get annoyed and leave. Remember the exit plan. I always have one. In the past, I became part of the chaos. Now those scenes remind me of why I don't want to or need to drink. They actually are a real deterrent for the desire to pick up. If you don't believe me give it a try. Go to a drinking party and stay sober and do not drink. Now try to have an intelligent conversation with someone after they have been slamming shots for a few hours. If you enjoyed the experience, then someone must have spiked your drink. For me, watching a bunch of drunks acting like fools is a living example of what I was and never want to be again.

Editorial Comment

A Double Standard

This is tough for me. Not everyone has this disease. Not everyone needs to refrain from drinking. I certainly am not favoring a return to prohibition. I encourage those who can handle a drink, to drink responsibly.

An organization I am associated with sends mixed messages to its employees with regards to alcohol. This organization has a premier substance abuse program. It provides yearly training to its employees on substance abuse. Weekend safety briefings constantly encourage responsible drinking. A DUI is generally a career ending offense. They openly encourage employees to seek help through counseling and REHAB. On the surface, it appears the organization is sending the right message.

I have seen many an employee destroy or severely hamper their career due to alcohol related incidents. I have sponsored a number of these individuals that could not break the grips of alcohol in this high stress environment. The wards in our local REHAB centers are filled with employees struggling with substance abuse issues. So, is there is another side to this story? I say yes, the same organization encourages the purchase and consumption of alcohol. Alcohol is sold at a discount at the organization sponsored liquor store; these stores are generically named the Class Six store. You see, alcohol is actually classified as a class of supply like food or truck parts. There are also convenience stores that are open on the grounds and many sell alcoholic beverages twenty four seven. So, if you need a drink on the way to work; on the way home; or at three in the morning, the convenience store is ready and waiting for you. I certainly took advantage of this service. In fact, approximately fifty percent of the floor space in my local organization sponsored convenience store is dedicated to alcohol. The tradition of the organizations sponsored bar is also alive and well. I see advertisements everyday on electronic billboards advertising the latest event at the organization watering hole. One of the two drinking establishments on the grounds allows you to purchase a mug which is proudly displayed behind the bar. Your mug is waiting for you to come in and enjoy your afternoon drinks prior to driving home. Everywhere you look, this fine organization is ready to serve.

Often at the convenience stores and the Class Six stores there are displays manned by eager salespersons giving us free samples of alcohol on the way home from work. Even commercial moonshine is for sale. I thought this organization that employs so many discouraged drinking and driving. I guess it is only an issue if you get caught. One day I entered the convenience store on the way home from work to pick up some milk and I was asked to sample some liquor they were pushing that day. I politely refused. The salesperson continued to push me to take the drink stating that it was cold outside and this was just what I needed to warm me up. It wasn't until I stated that I was a recovering alcoholic that the salesperson backed down. This is just one example of my concern with this organization's double standard. I frankly question the organization's commitment to its own substance abuse program. Just like many other workplaces, office Christmas and holiday parties happen. I receive flyers via my work e-mail with wonderful graphics. One I received not only encouraged heavy drinking, it glorified it. I personally like the graphic of the partygoer passed out on the floor. The gentleman with the lampshade on his head and a drink in each hand is certainly not sending the message for responsible drinking.

I am by no means saying that this organization should ban alcohol sales on its grounds. However, it should take a moment and ask itself, "Are we truly practicing what we preach or are we sending a mixed message?"

Using My Sentries to Prevent a Relapse

Concern over a relapse is often on the mind of this recovering alcoholic. Although I am deadly serious about never picking up a drink again, I understand that this disease is more powerful than my personal will. I understand that a tragic event or a series of setbacks in life could threaten my sobriety. Alcohol was for years my method to deal with adversity and an unexpected event could land me right back in the bottle. Also, just simple apathy or complacency could open me up for a relapse. I must thoroughly believe that my disease is patiently lying in wait for that moment of weakness and is ready and poised to pounce at the right moment of weakness, throwing me back into that endless cycle of misery and helplessness.

Knowing that challenge is awaiting me and also believing that these significant threats are a matter of when not if, I have decided to take action to prepare for this epic battle of the mind. I have drawn my analogy from my military background; I have called my plan of defense "My Sentries." I imagine in the Middle Ages there was a king who decided not to take the necessary steps to properly protect himself against his enemies. He did not build an adequate wall to keep out his enemies. He did not surround himself with personal guards and refused to spend the funds on a well trained and equipped army. The moat around the castle was probably too much trouble to dig and maintain. He was too busy to study his enemies and their intentions. The result was probably an invasion from an unexpected enemy resulting in him losing his throne or even his life. Even today, countries and important figures guard against threats and enemies. Imagine the President of the

United States of America deciding that he did not need the Secret Service and deciding to conduct his daily business out among the population with no concern of assassination. Most sane people would consider this decision foolhardy and possibly insane.

A recovering alcoholic would also be insane not to take the necessary steps to prevent a relapse. I surround myself with my sentries. The first line of defense is my fellows who I see at meetings and socialize with as often as possible. They are fellow alcoholics who have a common goal to remain sober. The second line of defense is the meetings I attend. These meetings remind me of who I was and how much I still need to learn each day. The third line of defense is the steps which, if I live them daily and make them part of my life, give me the armor against attack from my disease. The fourth line of defense is my service to others who are fighting the same battle as I. The fifth line of defense is staying away from old haunts. This is my castle walls and my moat. It keeps me far away from the people, places, and things that may tempt me to relapse. The sixth line of defense is my Big Book of Alcoholics Anonymous; it contains my daily battle plan. Together we form an impenetrable web of protection against a relapse. Finally, I have my higher power. He is the general on the battlefield who synchronizes all my defenses into a formidable army that is unbeatable. I am not the general in this war. When I was the general of my life, my life was a series of disasters or pending disasters. The general of my army, my higher power, is much better suited for the job. As long as I keep my army well taken care of, I will be prepared to face the challenge of a relapse. I will be prepared to defeat that inevitable mental assault that will push me to take that first drink.

Where is my parade?

When I got sober for real I naturally was feeling pretty good about myself. Never had I imagined that I could put down the bottle. I thought I was doomed to be a slave to alcohol until the day I died. I wanted everyone I knew to immediately notice how I overcame such a grave affliction. I wanted them to see how much work I put into changing my way of life. I expected constant praise and admiration. I wanted my parade with accolades and awards. *I should be put up on a pedestal and worshipped. Frank is the great Sober God! A savior of all that is wicked.* He is a grand example for all to follow. This again is an example of how dangerous alcoholic thinking can remain even after a period of sobriety. This is the exact thinking that will make me drink again.

To my disappointment and bewilderment there were no parades, awards, or worship. Everyone went on with their own lives. I guess I am not the center of the universe after all. Yes, there were people who supported me, but they weren't thinking about throwing me a party. Just the opposite was true. They were waiting and watching to see if this drunk would let them down as he has done so many times in the past. They hoped for the best, but expected the worst. I can't blame them because I am solely responsible for their feelings.

What I learned was even though I was sober, I still thought like an alcoholic. I still wanted to be the center of attention. I wanted to be the man. I was still playing God. I still haven't rid myself of this personal defect. I had to realize that being sober and living a selfless life was what I was supposed to be doing all along. You shouldn't get praise for what you are supposed to do.

Now occasionally someone will say they are proud of me or comment that I'm doing great. I appreciate the words of encouragement but ensure I keep it in perspective and not let it go to my head. I must remind myself that I am one drink away from being drunk again. The greatest gift of sobriety is sobriety itself. This gift brings me a real life with a real purpose.

Just for Fun

Are AA's Super Heroes?

It is a pretty bold statement to say AA's are Super Heroes since humility is such a critical part of recovery. Despite that fact, a case can be made, at least figuratively, for the Super Hero mantra being placed on active members of Alcoholics Anonymous. Let's look at the comparison.

Super Heroes
They fight their arch nemesis

AA's
We fight our arch nemesis – Alcohol

Super Heroes
They rescue people from their arch nemesis

AA's
We rescue new comers from Alcohol

Super Heroes
They live normal quiet lives and are always ready to perform their super hero duties.

AA's
We live normal quiet lives and are always ready to help another alcoholic in need.

Super Heroes
They do not look for or seek any public praise or reward for their work.

AA's
We do not look for or seek any public praise or reward for our work.

Super Heroes
They are humble and care only of helping others.

AA's
We are humble and care only of helping others.

Super Heroes
They each have a super power

AA's
We have a super power; our Higher Power

Super Heroes
They have super weapons

AA's
We have a super weapon; the Big Book

So, we should all come up with our super hero names but keep it to ourselves.

As a group we may want to call ourselves:

"The League of Extraordinary Sober People"

A Story I Heard from a Speaker at a Meeting

A drunk wakes up on the floor after a hard nights drinking. He looks around and is relieved that this time he is in his own living room. He scans the room with his foggy vision and notices a figure standing in the corner. As he focuses on this figure, he realizes it is GOD. As his eyes continue to clear he notices God is holding a shiny object in his hands. He say's "Hey God, what are you holding." God answers "Sobriety." The man states "Well God, I could sure use some of that Sobriety." God asks the Man "How much money do you have?" The man, a little taken back by the strange question, roots around in his pockets and finding fifty dollars states, "I've got fifty dollars." God says, "Give me the fifty dollars and I will give you this Sobriety." The man stumbles to his feet and staggers over to God and hands God the fifty dollars. As soon as God takes the money, the man begins to panic and says, "Excuse me God, but can I get twenty dollars back because I just remembered that I need gas for my car." God asks, "You have a car?" The man replies "yes, I need gas to get to work." God replies, "You have a job too? Well son, if you want this sobriety you have to give me your car and your job." The man states, "God, if you take my car and job, I won't be able to afford my house and family." God continues, "If you want this sobriety, I will have to take your house and your family too." The man is now completely frustrated and says, "God, if you take my money, car, job, house, and family, you are taking my entire life." God responds calmly and resolutely, "Yes son, if you want this sobriety, I you have to give me your life." Well, this drunk is at rock bottom and says, "God, take it all, take my life, just please give me sobriety." God hands the man the sobriety and the man instantly feels better. The man thanks God and turns and starts to humbly walk away. "Hold on" states God. The man turns around curious to see what God could possibly want from him now. God hands him the fifty dollars back and tells him to put gas in God's car. He then tells him to drive God's car to God's work and do God's job. He is to never drive God's car drunk and do God's job honestly and selflessly. He also tells him that he can live in God's house and take care of God's family as long as he takes care of the house and treats his family as God treats him. The man finally understands and lives his life according to God's will, not his own.

When I first heard this story, it was a spiritual awakening for me. Prior to that I never could fully grasp step three, "Turn your will and life over to the care of God as you understand him." It seemed like an impossible task and an unrealistic expectation. I now realize that all I needed to do was to conduct my life in accordance with my understanding of what God's will for me is and stop doing things my way and in accordance with my will. I found that giving up my will, which was not working anyway, I was gaining so much more than I could ever imagine. Don't tell God this, but I think he is getting the raw end of the bargain. He gets my crap and gives me his gold.

If I Had a Personal Mascot, I Would Choose Wile E. Coyote

A mascot represents the attitude or tone a group or team wants to portray. Clemson University has the Tigers. Chicago has the Bears. Most mascots are a strong and confident symbolic representation of the team. So it would be understandable to roll your eyes and wonder why this bumbling fool that is the antithesis of a mascot and the archetype of repeated failure could possibly be a good choice as my mascot. In this case, Wile E. Coyote does not represent what I aspire to be, but represents what I never want to be again.

Let's look at this iconic cartoon character that has entertained generations. The Road Runner cartoon has one basic premise. The Road Runner gleefully runs around the desert and the coyote attempts to catch and eat him. The coyote is obsessed with catching the Road Runner. No matter what he tries or what elaborate plan he devises, he fails to achieve his goal. In every episode the coyote crashes to the bottom of ravines, blows himself up, or is pounded by falling rocks. It is hilarious because everyone except him can see he will never achieve his goal to catch the Road Runner. A normal coyote would quit this insane endeavor and find another source of food.

This coyote suffers from a mental obsession. All he can think about is the satisfaction of catching and devouring the Road Runner. No matter how many disasters occur, how many cliffs he falls off of, or how many times he gets blown up by his own actions, he believes the next time will be different. Every other aspect of his life becomes second to his obsessive quest. He spends countless hours devising plans and procuring tools to get the Road Runner. He isolates himself and is blind to the world around him. He ignores his health and safety. Failure after failure, bottom after bottom does not deter him from his insane pursuit. Albert Einstein said "The definition of insanity is doing the same thing over and over again expecting different results." No one would doubt that the coyote is blindly, insanely, obsessed and will continue to hit bottom after bottom. His situation will get progressively worse never better unless he quits. I believe the coyote was not always insane and I now know from experience he can regain his sanity. The first time he saw that delicious meal racing across the desert he just saw it as a quick fix to his hunger. I can only assume he had tasted that fine meat before and wanted that satisfaction again. Something must have happened to the coyote during that first chase that didn't happen to other coyotes. His sickness grew from a desire to an obsession over a period of time. Finally, it must have overwhelmed him.

As I look back on my active alcoholic days of drinking, I see the coyote in me. Now sober, when I stumble on the cartoon I don't see the humor others see. I feel sorrow for the coyote. I see a reflection of me as I once was.

Yes, the coyote is the perfect mascot for me. It is a reminder of not triumph, but of tragedy.

Balance

I believe I have adequately made the case that alcohol destroyed all balance in my life as an active alcoholic. When alcohol was the number one priority, all other loves, desires, and responsibilities instantly became a distant second. And when I did address those priorities, the effort was a half-step due to the fog of alcohol. One goal of sobriety is to get balance back in your life. I did a poor job finding that critical balance early in my sobriety. I rightly poured every free moment in that critical first year into my sobriety. I attended meetings every day and engulfed myself reading everything I could get my hands on reference living a clean and sober life. I volunteered for service work at my local AA club and I maintained my sobriety. I simply put as much effort into staying sober as I committed to being a drunk.

The problem was I never started the transition from the total focus on staying sober to finding that balance in life that was lost in my drunkenness. In a way I replaced one addiction with another addiction. Although my life was not deadly and destructive, it was still totally out of balance. After a year I should have consciously begun to incorporate what I learned and work equally hard at finding a full and balanced life in sobriety. This mistake almost cost me my marriage. I am not suggesting that I should have abandoned the program of recovery that saved my life. I am saying that I should have done a better job taking those lessons and using them in all aspects of my interpersonal life. I now realize that it is critical that anyone in recovery should be fully reintegrated into the society they live in.

Now my focus is on finding that critical balance. I still work my recovery daily. I go to meetings two to three times a week; I do my service work; and I live the principles of the program daily. I also am fully integrated into my family life, work life, and community. As I continue to heal, I strive to be a productive member of this world.

John Barleycorn

I have tried to understand what Jack London was saying is his novel "John Barleycorn", a novel that shocked the world in 1913. He was a beloved author famed for classic novels such as "White Fang" and "The Call of the Wild" and then subsequently published a book that chronicled his battle with alcohol. This hero of prose revealed his dark underbelly for the entire world to see. Dark, adventurous, and often disturbing, it outlined his life long battle with alcohol. Written in a lost form of English with words that are rarely spoken and can only be found at championship rounds at spelling bees, it can be a difficult read. The word dipsomaniac is the term that was the precursor to the current term of alcoholic and is an example of the words of that long lost day.

This is my interpretation of Mr London's message coupled with my personal experience. I believe Jack understood, but never escaped the abyss of alcohol. Although the cause of his untimely death is debated, his use of alcohol clearly was a contributing factor. I see this as a must read for all who are struggling with the disease.

The interpretation is written using the terms and phrases of the time with current terms in parentheses.

If a dipsomaniac (alcoholic) comes to understand the white logic (The brutal truth as seen through the eyes of an alcoholic) and by doing so walks with and is imprisoned by the noseless one (skull/death), then he is doomed to the slow suicide that only John Barleycorn (alcohol) brings. But, if he survives the descending abyss (my reference) and puts John Barleycorn behind him, he can embrace and transcend the inescapable truth of the white logic. He can then understand and even master the noseless one. From that point on, he can embrace life, death, and all that lies between. For those who never travelled that horrific path and walk through life in a form of ignorant bliss, I am not sure if I am jealous of them; grateful that they sidestepped the abyss; or feel just a sense of spiritual detachment from them. The true sadness I feel is for those who fall into the abyss; walk with the noseless one; live in fear of what the white logic brings; and finally falls into the blackness and never returns.

The sadness of the novel is Jack London understood the disease, wrote about it in this novel and many of his other works, but could not call himself a real alcoholic. This was his ultimate demise as is the case with many alcoholics today. He felt he could think his way out of this disease. He admitted that the disease was primarily mental yet he felt intelligent enough to overcome the disease on his own. At age forty, three years after the publication of the novel he succumbed to the ravages of alcohol.

My life in Recovery

Is it really as good as they say?

I give it a resounding yes. I am truly amazed that life in recovery is better than I could have ever imagined. Just the fact that I don't ever have to worry about getting a DUI or going to jail because alcohol was running the show is a relief. I don't have to worry about alcohol taking my job, my marriage, my family, my house, my self-esteem, and of course my life. But that is only the beginning. I am actively involved in a fellowship of recovering and recovered people like me and draw strength from them and hopefully they do from me in turn. I have the opportunity now to help others who are suffering with this horrible and unforgiving disease. I am becoming the person I have always wanted to be. I am changing into the person that my parents would be proud of and my children want to look up to. I am becoming the rock my wife always wanted and deserved in her life. I can smile and really mean it. Words like peace of mind and serenity actually apply in my life.

I am not saying that life is perfect. Life still comes at me on life's terms. The difference is I am now clear headed and I can deal with life's twists and turns calmly. I have a higher power that is with me to get me through any challenge. I don't drink over life or try to drink it away. Things I can't totally handle, I give over to my higher power and somehow I get through it. I no longer live a life of constant chaos. I don't drown in self-pity and resentment. I can now look at myself in the mirror and like what I see.

What truly amazes me is I am no longer a selfish person who has to have everything his way on his terms. Oh, that selfish bastard is in there, ready to come out at any moment, but I strive to be selfless in all things I do. I choose to no longer be the center of my own personal universe. I do not hurt others, and if I do, I quickly make amends and fix my behavior. I regret my past deeds but do not dwell on them. I try to learn from them instead. I no longer worry about the future. I live for today and I am happy.

"JUST FOR TODAY"

And That's all Right with Me

I Hope my Epitaph Reads:

Frank K
A Drunk Who
Decided Not To
Drink, He Died With
Dignity - Sober

Bibliography

Co-founders. Alcoholics Anonymous, Fourth Edition. New York, New York. Alcoholics Anonymous World Services, INC, 2001: pages 62,63, 86-93, 94, 151

Co-founders. Twelve Steps and Twelve Traditions. New York, New York. Alcoholics Anonymous World Services, INC, 2001: page 94

Co-Founder. As Bill Sees it. New York, New York. Alcoholics Anonymous World Services, INC, 2001: page 94

Jack London. John Barleycorn, Post Falls, Idaho. Century Publishing, 1913: pages 163-164

Acknowledgments

I would like to give thanks to my beautiful wife Theresa who has supported me throughout my journey to sobriety. My children Savannah, Lauren, Larry, Erin, Frankie, and Luke, for their understanding and support. A Special thanks to the leadership team Ken, Wes, Tom, and Steve at Fort Knox for supporting me through my rehabilitation and ensuring my job was waiting for me upon my return. Thanks to Sharon for your editing assistance. To my good friends Donna and Brenda for always lending a sympathetic ear. Finally, to all my fellow recovering and recovered alcoholics who walk this journey with me every day I am forever in your debt.

Printed in the United States
By Bookmasters